Fine Points of FURNITURE

Fine Points of FURNITURE

EARLY AMERICAN

By ALBERT SACK

Foreword by
ISRAEL SACK

Introduction by
JOHN MEREDITH GRAHAM II
Former Curator, Colonial Williamsburg

NEW YORK
CROWN PUBLISHERS, INC.

ISBN 0-517-001489
Manufactured in the United States Of America

30 29 28 27 26 25

To my dear wife, May,

and

To my father, Israel Sack, who, in his forty-seven years of dealing in Early American antiques, has captured the true spirit of the greatness of the American character as reflected in our finest furniture and is responsible for the proper direction of a number of the most notable public and private collections of seventeenth and eighteenth century American furniture.

ACKNOWLEDGMENT

IN THE selection of the photographs used in this book, I was rewarded by the enthusiastic cooperation of a number of dealers, museums, private collectors, and other sources. Among the dealers, David Stockwell, Joe Kindig, Jr., and John K. Byard, of Silvermine Tavern, opened their extensive files for my unlimited use. The files of Israel Sack, Inc., were the nucleus from which I began the selection, and they yielded a large number of the photographs used. Other dealers who provided photographs were: John Walton, Hyman Grossman, William Richmond, Lester Berry, Leon David, John Schwartz, I. Winick, and P. E. Millman. The photography firm of Taylor and Dull, which handles the files of Parke-Bernet Auction Galleries, proved a rich source, and James Pennypacker, auctioneer, sent me a whole carton of accumulated pictures.

I would like to thank Miss Alice Winchester, editor of *Antiques,* who generously extended full use of the files of the magazine; Erwin O. Christansen, Director of the Index of American Design, National Gallery of Art, for his cooperation and for permitting the use of a number of photographs; and Sidney Rutman and Dexter Spaulding of the Old Colony Furniture Company. The kind assistance of Hayward S. Ablewhite, Director of the Edison Institute, in opening the vast files of this extensive museum for my selection resulted in a considerable number of valuable photographs; and a number of select pictures were used from the Karolik Collection in the Boston Museum of Fine Arts. The great majority of the photographs used in this book are of pieces in private collections and most of them have never before been published.

FOREWORD

I AM doubly proud of my son for his accomplishment in writing this book. First, is the natural pride of a father who sees his son carry on his life's work of preaching the importance of Early American craftsmanship. But I am also proud because his novel presentation of the subject is clear, simple, and instructive.

My earliest recollections of the American antique business date back to forty-seven years ago in Boston. At that time I was working in an antique store repairing furniture for the fine old families of Beacon Hill and also for the dealers and collectors. Having learned the cabinetmaker's trade in Lithuania, such terms as Queen Anne, Chippendale, Hepplewhite, etc., meant nothing to me. But as I worked on the fine American pieces which came into the shop for repair, I became very attached to them. I did not care who made them or how old they were, but from a cabinetmaker's standpoint they appealed to me as having stately lines and a quality for which I soon developed a deep and sincere attachment.

Even though things were sold cheaply compared to today's prices, one could not expect to buy much from the margin of ten-dollar-a-week wages. I realize now that my desire for handling and acquiring some of those fine pieces gave me incentive to work hard so that I could accumulate money to deal in them. If it had not been for my appreciation of American antiques, I should probably never have gone into business for myself as quickly as I did.

I arrived in this country on the fifteenth of November, 1903. By July, 1905, I had started in my own business. I began by repairing furniture for other dealers and collectors. Here it was that I came in contact with fine pieces which they had bought in the rough and wanted repaired. Time meant nothing to me in those days. I was only twenty-one; and besides starting to work at six every morning, I spent my evenings and Sundays visiting the antique scouts.

They traveled about during the day, and did most of their selling at night and on Sundays. Inasmuch as this was before the era of the automobile, some of them would hire a horse and buggy and start out from Boston. They would work within a radius of twenty-five or thirty miles, at times staying away for a whole week. Those who were less fortunate would go either on foot or by streetcar, generally keeping within about five miles of the city. When they returned in the evening, they opened their places and sold by candlelight.

It was interesting to listen to some of the experiences that these fellows had on their excursions. Generally, after the purchaser had spent about thirty minutes in buying something, he lingered a few hours more listening to the stories they had to tell.

Each scout had a few dealers and collectors to whom he sold. The scouts and small dealers then looked up to collectors; they considered it an honor to sell to a well-known collector like the late Eugene Bolles, who was quite a character himself. The small dealers and the few scouts were then considered to be more in the class of second-hand furniture and junk dealers who occasionally found a good piece.

A great many of the collectors were inexperienced. The majority of them were influenced by a few of the earlier collectors, but they were always afraid of being wrongly guided. Whatever price a dealer asked they thought exhorbitant. They were sincere in this, however; and in the majority of cases they absolutely refused to buy, much to their regret later.

After the Krim sale, the next great event which happened in the American antique field to influence new buyers was the Hudson Fulton Exhibition, held in New York from September 25 until October 11, 1907. Mr. Bolles, probably the foremost early collector, exhibited practically his entire collection. Later Mrs. Russell Sage purchased and presented this collection to the Metropolitan Museum.

Up to that time the Museum had exhibited

mostly foreign furniture, whether good, bad, or indifferent. This was not the fault of the Museum or its trustees, but was because it was very difficult in those days to purchase anything American inasmuch as very few of our wealthier people cared anything about Americana. Few people realized what wonderful furniture had been made in this country by the early settlers. Mrs. Russell Sage's purchase and presentation of the Bolles collection to the Museum was the turning point.

The earliest collectors of Americana deserve much credit. They were not people of means when they started collecting. It was at a great sacrifice to themselves that most of them purchased their antiques, even though the prices would now seem ridiculously low. Even as late as 1910 a few of the collectors whom I knew were buying fine Americana at a great sacrifice to themselves. They never would have done it had they not appreciated the beauty of the pieces..

Besides sacrificing comforts and luxuries to acquire rare pieces, many people were accused of having gone wrong in the upper story, and were called "antique bugs" and even "junk collectors."

The idea of buying antiques for actual use in homes was a new one which people of ordinary means knew nothing of. The word "antique" was associated with museums or with persons who had palaces in which to house them. The simple New England pieces, however, were not made for palaces. They were built by fine cabinetmakers who came here from England, Holland, and other European countries; and, naturally, the workers from England were influenced by the Jacobean, Queen Anne, and other period styles of English furniture. There were marvelous cabinetmakers among them.

The furniture now displayed in museums and private collections is sufficient evidence that a number of them were great masters who worked into their furniture a combination of fine craftsmanship and durability, and a wonderful sensitiveness to woods which, after one hundred years of usage, have blended together giving the pieces a charm which no new piece can have. Even though a piece were made as well today—and this is almost an impossibility, not because there are no fine cabinetmakers but because of the difference in our standard of living which demands that everything be done in a hurry—very few persons would be willing to pay a high price for something which would last one hundred and fifty or two hundred years. Furniture constructed in the same manner and with the same care today, would, in most cases, cost more money than people are paying for the old.

The finest furniture in America was made between the years 1680 and 1820. Persons of wealth and social position filled their homes with the best furniture that the most skillful craftsmen could create for them, as this tasteful and careful furnishing was one of the few ways in which families of means could display their wealth and indicate their hospitality to their distinguished guests.

As the eighteenth century progressed, craftsmen grew in numbers, as did also families with means to build and furnish fine homes. As the country became larger and more prosperous it acquired a feeling of self-sufficiency and the people began to place more confidence in their native craftsmen. There was growing up a new generation with no recollections of Europe.

The cabinetmaking industry flourished here from that time to the beginning of the nineteenth century. It had taken a long time for the descendants of the early settlers to realize that things could be done as well in this country as abroad. The best American furniture was made prior to 1820, after which time machinery was brought into use. Until the coming of the "machine age" almost everything had been done by hand, and every good cabinetmaker was trained so that he could create his pieces practically from the log to the finished product.

The idea which some people have—that antiques are valuable merely because of their age—is wrong. No matter how old a piece may be, it has no value unless it is of good quality. Age is really a secondary matter where antiques are concerned. Of prime consideration are the quality of the article, the design and the maker, the fineness and durability of the woods, and a mellowness imparted to them by a hundred or more years of natural wear, which no human hand can duplicate and no dyes imitate. Persons who place too much stress on the fact that their possessions are old are often greatly disappointed and unable to understand when they find that their things are valueless.

Not long ago a man spent one hundred dollars advertising a clock, which was only worth five dollars but for which he wanted twenty-five thousand dollars. He maintained that he would not have thought of selling it except that he wanted to retire a mortgage on his farm and send a few of his children to college. Recently I received a communication from a man who was willing to part with an heirloom for forty thousand dollars. Forty dollars, however, would have been a high price for it. There are thousands of such cases where people think that they are wealthy because they possess a few old beds or old pine chests which were made by the thousands and put in barns to hold grain.

If you go to the root of the evil in the antique trade, buyers who are not well treated, or who find that the article they purchased is not as good as they thought, are really as much to blame as the dealer. It is a fifty-fifty proposition. I have read most of the articles in which collectors are warned about "getting stuck." They are apt to be written by people who have never purchased any antiques of merit, either because they could not afford the finer things, or because they insist on looking for bargains. Buyers who try to take advantage of dealers, and are always looking for new ones who have not yet learned the business and are unaware of the value of the articles they are selling, are the very ones who send out S. O. S. warnings to all interested in antiques to beware of imitations.

There are fundamental principles governing all business. If you follow them you cannot be fooled. Bargains are expensive. No matter what you buy as a "bargain," in most cases it is not actually a bargain. In every line of business there are merchants who understand human nature almost as well as Barnum did, and who therefore realize that bargain-hunters multiply so fast that in order to cater to that class of trade it is necessary to create imaginary bargains. And there are buyers in every line who are not satisfied unless their purchases are procured at a bargain. In some cases they succeed, but in the majority they do not.

There is, of course, more than one reason why dealers try to imitate antiques to fool buyers; and more than one reason why people will buy them. Someone once remarked that in order to have honest politicians the people themselves must be honest. For every man who accepts a bribe, there is always someone to offer one. For every seller of spurious or misrepresented articles, there is always a buyer who is willing to take advantage of someone. I do not doubt that in a good many cases buyers of imitations know that they are not paying for the genuine article, but only feel hurt when someone tells them. Some buyers who have the means do it because they are not willing to pay the price for the real thing; and those who cannot afford the real—but like good things—buy on the chance of finding a bargain.

I am personally acquainted with some of the best buyers of Americana. They are not fooled merely because they do not take chances; they are not looking for bargains.

Now let us take the other side—why people make up these pieces to sell. Surely it is not the way to build up business and gain the confidence of buyers.

Today there is, of course, the excuse that the genuine article is scarce, high-priced, and costs more than most dealers are willing to invest in one item. But, in comparison to the number of dealers and buyers then and now, there was more faking going on twenty-five years ago than there is today. The question is, why do they fake when there is so much of the old on the market?

The answer is that some dealers are not satisfied with any transaction unless they can put something over, even though they could make more money legitimately. They do it for the sport and thrill of the thing. There has been—and still is—a common expression in the trade, that some buyers deserve to get stuck; and some dealers enjoy leaving nothing undone in order that the buyer may get what he deserves.

When I was working at the bench repairing antiques, there were generally two or three dealers around the shop talking over the different shady transactions they had put across. They would tell customers stories about the poor old lady who cried when she had to part with pieces which had belonged to her great, great grandfather: an oak chest, for example. In those days oak chests were re-carved by the hundreds and sold as fast as they were carved. It was much more difficult to buy a genuine piece than it is now. The reason lay in the fact that people were not interested in antiques unless they either had some story connected with them or were beautifully polished up.

When cabinetmakers did repairing for people they frequently did not return the original, but made a duplicate from old wood and then boasted that they had made the old look just like new. It was much easier for dealers to make an article out of old wood than to go through the country and search for old ones, always a difficult task requiring a lot of time and patience. Moreover, one had to be a born trader to induce the old New England families to part with their heirlooms, especially at the low prices which the scouts were willing to pay.

The finest pieces had to be taken apart, scraped and finished inside and out before they could be sold to people who were not collectors of the Bolles type. Bolles was always satisfied to leave his things in the rough, for he appreciated the value of the old. Innumerable choice pieces were absolutely ruined by poor restoration. There is nothing which hurts an early oak piece so much as planing, scraping, and finishing. Mahogany and walnut, when properly restored, are not necessarily spoiled. But, although planing and scraping cannot take away the age of pine, oak, or maple, they do kill all their charm, and hence their resale value.

Museums are criticized for having their pieces restored. The purpose of a museum, however, is educational. The articles are not for sale, and a certain amount of restoration is necessary in order to show them as they originally were. For private collectors who purchase with the idea of reselling at some future date, it is, of course, advisable to buy things as nearly original as possible.

Many persons are worried about the future of the antique business. They are afraid that prices will go so high that few people will be able to buy. A gentleman recently told me that in a paper printed in 1908 he had read an article, written by a dealer, which complained of the scarcity and prices of antiques. The antique business, however, has grown continually until it has become an established business in which intelligent people are investing millions of dollars.

Dealers would not invest hundreds of thousands of dollars in antiques if they had no confidence in the future of the business. The law of supply and demand governs antiques as well as everything else. As things become more scarce, they will naturally increase in price. The demand is continually growing for better things, not because people have more money now, but because buyers have become more educated. They have better means of learning than they had twenty-five years ago. Dealers, as well as collectors, have learned something and are better able to advise their customers.

After my forty-odd years in the antique business I feel that there are very few businesses equal to it. Aside from the money one can make in it—which is not one-half of one percent of what can be made in some other businesses by persons of no greater ability—it is interesting because of its endless variety both in the people whom the dealer meets and the pieces which he handles. It is one of the few businesses left which cannot be standardized. It gives one a great thrill to discover and purchase a rare item, and a great deal of pleasure to sell it to the right person. One comes into contact with the finest people in America.

Seventy-five percent of all the antiques I have handled during the last forty-five years have been bought from dealers. I have found that very few of them try to fool me. As a class, I enjoy doing business with them. If I had it to do all over again, I think that I should prefer the antique business to any other.

There are those who do not care anything about the special historical significance of an old piece of furniture, china, or silver. They do not feel that this adds to its value, and are not willing to pay more for it for that reason. Still others care nothing about the quality of the article itself as long as it has associations with noted personages. My own position in the matter is that, although I consider that historical significance adds to the interest of the piece, I should not buy it unless it also had merit and were useful. If an article of fine quality likewise has an interesting and absolutely authentic history, I should consider it priceless for anyone who could afford to own it.

There is romance associated with all old American things inasmuch as the country was comparatively new when they were made and most of their owners had to fight for mere existence. If they did not actually fight the Indians or the elements, they at least had to struggle to become established in the new country. Only a small percent of the early settlers could afford to have furniture of quality. These fine old things are now rare and becoming more so all the time.

I consider it a privilege for persons to be able to own the few distinguished pieces which have come down to us from the signers of the Declaration of Independence or the generals of the Revolution, especially since these things can still be used in homes today. We would not, of course, want to wear the clothes or shoes of these illustrious persons, but we can live with their furniture; and I believe that such pieces, when their history is absolutely authentic, should bring at least five times as much as an article of the same quality but without the historical association.

The only kind of piece that I should consider authentic historically is one whose origin and history can be proven beyond any reasonable doubt. Almost every family is willing to give to articles which they possess a history that cannot be traced, but the percentage of authentic historical pieces is very small. I never even quote these doubtful stories after I have purchased the pieces. I have, however, handled a number of absolutely authentic historical pieces.

What will happen when more wealthy people will begin to realize that this country produced as fine furniture as any made in any other land? Who can predict, as my collector friend did in 1914, that prices of fine American antiques will never go higher? More and more museums are preserving and appreciating American-made pieces. The market is getting larger, and the rare pieces come to light more infrequently. It is not an isolated condition. If you consider the recent development and awakened interest in American literature, painting, architecture, and music, it is not hard to see that we are merely on the threshold of a great new era.

Israel Sack

September, 1950
New York, N. Y.

CONTENTS

INTRODUCTION

For the collector of today, a vast amount of work has already been accomplished in determining what is American furniture and how it differs from European examples. Although this constitutes an excellent foundation, a great deal of research still remains to be done in various regional areas of the United States before a comprehensive picture can be presented. Full treatment of the subject must await the publication of books now in the process of being written and others that will be undertaken in the future on furniture from sections of the country about which little is known at the present time.

A debt of gratitude is due the first American writer on the subject, Mr. Luke Vincent Lockwood, dean of the field, for his two volumes, *Colonial Furniture in America*. This outstanding and scholarly contribution is being continued by Mr. Joseph Downs, now Curator of The Henry Francis du Pont Museum, Winterthur, Delaware, and formerly Curator of the American Wing of the Metropolitan Museum.

Private collectors have played no less a part than the writers in creating a new era in the appreciation of the history of American furniture. Since the turn of the century, many outstanding collections have become available either through public auction or as presentations to art museums, and these have left a marked impression on the American public. The dispersal of the Howard Reifsnyder collection some twenty years ago startled the country by the prices obtained for American specimens, while the auction sale in 1944 of Mrs. J. Amory Haskell's vast assemblage set a new record for the most extensive collection brought together in our time by one individual. The restoration of Colonial Williamsburg—containing eighty old buildings and three hundred reconstructed edifices with a detailed study of social aspirations, living conditions, excavated artifacts, the use of eighteenth century colors and related detail material—has captured the imagination of the entire nation. Its influence has not only contributed toward improving the general taste of the country in architectural designs for small houses and in decorative arts but it has set a practical precedent for the restoration of other colonial and early republic sites and buildings.

In early America there was by no means a lack of skilled native-born and European-trained craftsmen. The furniture designs of these men as well as their other useful arts were strongly influenced by changes in English fashions, but they were not mere provincial copies of London examples. The process of American individual development is evident in the artisans' rejection of stylistic vagaries that were alien to their temperament and to that of their customers. In turn the European-trained craftsman working in this country was so influenced by the American trend that his products soon began to conform to that of his locality. Two outstanding developments in American furniture are reflected in the highboy and the block-front which reached a height of perfection not equaled in any other country.

The satisfying appeal of good American furniture is based on honesty of line and distinction of design that has withstood, and gained added recognition by, the critical test of time. In part, this may be accounted for by the nature of the American market, where the best quality of furniture was made for prosperous men of affairs who demanded simplicity and dignity in their furnishings and eschewed the foppery of contemporary Europe. The tendency to cover up weak structural forms with superfluous ornamentation was minimized as a result. American craftsmen also reflected in their works the historical events of their respective times and were influenced by the fight to conquer a wilderness, recurrent wars, and a shifting struggle of conflicting groups and ideas. The self-assured ruling class of the South and the powerful mercantile interest of the North, the restless adventurers pushing westward to new frontiers beyond the confining Appalachian range, inventions of labor-saving devices, the translation of national resources into monetary wealth, and an abundance of new kinds of wood were contributory factors to the formation of the story of American furniture.

In England there was a different kind of market. The finest furniture was made by skilled craftsmen for the nobility who preferred elaborate designs. As a result, overornamentation was often stressed to the detriment of line and proportion. The simple English furniture was usually made by lesser cabinetmakers for the middle and lower classes who could not afford a costly product.

During the eighteenth century when decorative arts reached their highest point of perfection there was an assembling and refining of borrowed designs by both France and England from other sources. The dominant position in the world of fashion was held by France in dress as well as in furnishings and the changes in French styles were closely followed by England. The early study of the ordered Italian Renaissance resulted in a tendency to replace vertical forms with horizontal forms, and the introduction of the Flemish scroll into England along with caning from the Orient via Portugal as well as other Oriental influences were reflected in America chiefly by way of England.

The collecting instinct seems to be a universal trait, with practically everyone accumulating something, whether it is a series of business establishments, race horses, sea shells, or antiques. An added impetus was given to collecting during the last World War, when a scarcity of new furniture inadvertently turned a purchaser into a potential collector. As a result, prices reached prodigious heights, often without relation to quality or period of the object. A Victorian sofa was known to bring fifteen hundred dollars and a pair of vases of the same vintage six hundred. This type of buying could only mean that an "uninformed" group of collectors had arisen to plunge into an unfamiliar field without sufficent information.

There is no easy method of learning the art of collecting, and everyone makes the usual number of mistakes. However, time and money may be saved by beginners if more effort is devoted to reading some of the current publications relating to their respective interests before they begin to buy objects. It is also necessary to develop a trained eye and a critical point of view, which can best be acquired by seeing as many examples as possible. In general, new collectors are much better informed than their predecessors and usually avoid the obvious pitfall of starting with late periods only to find that later their tastes have changed to earlier forms and a new beginning has to be made.

Today it is not enough to know that an example is of a specific period, for there is an additional interest in determining the regional origin and, if possible, to what craftsman it may be attributed. The most important factor of all is whether an example is good of its kind and how it compares with similar types.

A book on comparatives was an essential need in the field and it was inevitable that eventually it would be written. The subject has been undertaken for the first time by Albert Sack, under the title *Fine Points of Furniture,* with a good, better, best comparison. This publication will provide an instructive guide for the general collector and a medium through which the advanced student may verify his standard of taste.

John Meredith Graham II
Curator of Collections
Colonial Williamsburg
Williamsburg, Virginia

Fine Points
of
FURNITURE

COLLECTING ANTIQUES

THERE has been more hocus-pocus and less common sense written and spoken about the lure of antiques than perhaps about any other subject. This is especially true since there is no logical method of categorizing, or of attempting to standardize, objects of art. By their very nature, each must be unique. Many who would like to collect antiques give up in disgust at the many contradictions they observe in the literature on the subject and among the collectors themselves. Many more, otherwise logical, persons spend considerable sums building collections of little or no merit by concentrating on the wrong values.

There is, however, one key and one key only to collecting antiques—quality. Neither age nor rarity nor historic association can be considered until the test of quality has been satisfied. Every successful collector has learned this lesson (many the hard way). Most people who collect improperly do so because they seek the secondary attributes without considering the essential merit of the piece. Too often the rarity of an item is emphasized to excuse its lack of other virtues. For example, a seven-spindled Windsor chair is very rare, but I would still choose a conventional nine-spindled Windsor if it had finer turnings and workmanship. In other words, rarity increases the value of a piece only if the basic superior qualities already exist. Naturally, if a gifted craftsman created a new form that was completely harmonious—and was the only one who accomplished this feat—those few surviving examples of this important type would be greatly sought after and highly prized. And among the American classics those types that were made in lesser number than others are naturally rarer and more valuable. Below this top level of quality, however, rarity rapidly diminishes in importance until it becomes something to be shunned.

In the theory of evolution it is stipulated that successful experiments are repeated while those that are unsuccessful are not. The latter never become important until they are practically extinct, and then only to demonstrate how Mother Nature herself can go off on a tangent. Or, let us consider something more closely allied with antiques—a Rembrandt painting. There are more Rembrandt paintings in existence today than there are paintings of several other less capable Dutch artists of the same period. Is Rembrandt less rare then? And, assuming that he is less rare than Van Ravesteyn, a contemporary of his, why do the latter's paintings bring only a fraction of the price of a Rembrandt? Obviously because Rembrandt was a genius, able to capture the greatness of his era and interpret it in his paintings. The *quality* of his masterpieces accounts for their great value. As a matter of fact, the value of one genuine Rembrandt painting can be far greater than that of another, for even masters can have off days. The true rarity is quality produced by genius, whether it be furniture, painting, or any other art or craft form.

The purpose of this book is to bring into focus the standards of quality in the phase of art with which I am most familiar—Early American furniture of the seventeenth and eighteenth centuries.

It was my good fortune to inherit a brilliant father who used his remarkable abilities in this particular field during the pioneer days of collecting Americana. When he came to Boston in 1903 and went to work as an apprentice cabinetmaker, he saw and repaired some of the great treasures which had been handed down in the noted Boston families. At that time these masterpieces were appreciated by few outside their owners, and sometimes not even by them. That was the time that Eugene Bolles, a lawyer of limited means but of great enthusiasm, could be considered queer and incompetent for forming the collection which later became the nucleus of the American Wing of the Metropolitan Museum of Art. He, Dwight Blaney, Luke Vincent Lockwood, and a few others were able to separate the wheat from the chaff.

The gap in price between the gems and the mediocre which today appears ludicrously small seemed colossal then. I enjoy particularly the story my father tells of a Pilgrim chair which he was offering to one of the early collectors. He asked sixty dollars for it. The collector became so angry at this "fantastic" price that his face became fiery red, but he finally succumbed. Since that time the same chair has been resold for well over a thousand dollars and is recognized as a priceless gem. My father has never tolerated mediocrity, and his enthusiasm for the truly great early American craftsmen has been responsible for the proper direction of many of the foremost collections of early American furniture.

When I joined my father in the antique business in 1934, this axiom of quality had already been proved during the first generation of collecting Americana, and I was provided with ample experience to help me avoid the usual pitfalls. However, I began to realize that every source of information available to the new collector tends to confuse rather than to clarify his goal. The extensive literature on the subject parades illustrations of examples of various periods with little or no effort made to select items of uniform excellence. Most of the popular books on antiques illustrate a large number of pieces which, because of the mediocrity in their design and construction, would not interest any serious collector. These inferior pieces are so intermingled with the masterpieces that they acquire a false prestige which, in turn, sends many a novice off on an unfortunate tangent.

Many people shy away from the word "collector." They say they are not in that class but they do like the atmosphere of antiques in their home and want to pick up a few. If a person buys an "antique" and it costs no more than the price of a new piece, no one is hurt and he probably has fun until his "antique" falls apart. But, when anyone acquires an antique and pays many times the price of a corresponding new piece, he is a collector in spite of himself and might as well collect intelligently. For, in my experience, with very few exceptions, no matter how avid an Americana collector may be, his primary concern is furnishing his home, and he will forego any fine piece which will not fit into his scheme. Antique furniture is not put into a glass case but is acquired only if it can be utilized, with the exception of certain few specimen pieces which were functional in former centuries but no longer are.

I have a great reverence for the products of the gifted craftsmen of the colonies and therefore I am sensitive to what I consider a misdirected passion for crudity in respect to Americana. In the national game known as "antiqueing," otherwise normal people ravenously devour the backwash of bygone days at the country auctions and antique shops that cover the countryside. Let this not be called a blanket condemnation of either auctions or antique shops, only of the refuse which has been known to drift into both. This glorifying of backwoods products in Americana is so prevalent that it has become an important trend in home decoration. According to this trend, American furniture is most adaptable to the kitchen, porch, or bedroom, where its crudity is charming, but never err by letting it invade the living or dining room —that is reserved for the sophisticated English or French cousins. Well, I wish to register as a small voice crying in the wilderness. Let me try to convince you that the American eighteenth century culture created its own dynamic and unique contributions to Art's permanent Hall of Fame and certainly need not apologize to England or any other country for its origin or its scope. In fact, many lovers of fine Americana, as well as I, sincerely believe that several schools of American craftsmanship, such as the New England Queen Anne, the Philadelphia Chippendale, and the Goddard-Townsend far surpassed the best English or French by their originality of form, elimination of frills and extraneous detail, as well as by their superb craftsmanship. I believe many Americans have an inferiority complex regarding our own arts. True, they may see some of our superb masterpieces in museums but those, they feel, are merely imitations of the English by craftsmen who migrated here.

Were American craftsmen creators or merely imitators? While the essential principles of structure and design are the same the world over, individual interpretation of beauty is infinitely varied and considerably influenced by environment. What seems beautiful to us might have no appeal to an Abyssinian; the Grecian Venus would have to cut down on her calories to qualify in Hollywood. The furniture made in this country in the seventeenth and eighteenth centuries need not be compared with English or French products to evaluate its merit. It has often been said that American antiques are merely imitations of the English, but the fact is that they differ only as much as the two countries and their inhabitants differed from one another. True, all influence on us originated in England, but it is just as true that this influence indirectly reflected the work and forms of many other countries and eras. Chippendale adapted designs from the Chinese, the French, Gothic architecture, and many others. It is said that few, if any, of Shakespeare's plots were original—they were adapted from works of previous authors. Does this make him less great? Just as his interpretations of old stories made him immortal, so America's interpretations of English designs provided original contributions.

However, since the principles underlying the construction of fine furniture were, and are, the same in all countries, it is unfair to compare the finest output of English cabinetmakers with the rural furniture of the Colonies, which many people think of when American antiques are mentioned. There is as much difference between a Goddard kneehole desk and a Vermont maple bureau as there is between a piece made in Chippendale's shop and one made on a farm in Yorkshire. From the standpoint of cabinetmaking, a piece produced by Goddard, Randolph, or Duncan Phyfe is certainly as fine as the greatest English creation. One should compare the beauty, originality, vigor, and the spirit of independence which made eighteenth century America great and which is reflected in its finest furniture. It can only be fully understood by those who appreciate the American spirit.

I maintain that we revere our cottage furniture because of the mistaken belief that it was our greatest contribution. We like to think of our early settlers living in log cabins and hewing their furniture from the trees surrounding their huts. But the evidence belies this conception. Thousands of magnificent colonial structures which are still standing and thousands more which have since been destroyed all contained furniture in keeping with their sophistication. During colonial days there were few ways to make use of wealth except in the home and its furnishings, providing the main reason for the great flowering of furniture craftsmanship and design. There was a substantial wealthy class in each of the important cities at one time or another during the seventeenth and eighteenth centuries, in Boston, Salem, Newport, Philadelphia, New York, Baltimore; and in hundreds of smaller towns of which Hartford, New Haven, Newburyport, Portsmouth and Dover, New Hampshire, Albany and Lancaster were but a few. In these and others too numerous to mention there was produced excellent furniture for the more affluent inhabitants. None of these fine urban homes contained cottage furniture. On the contrary, every item was ordered individually, with exacting specifications as to selection of well-seasoned lumber, careful construction, and fine detail. The craftsman was an honored member of his community, and several attained great wealth.

A surprising proportion of this superb furniture has survived in excellent condition. It is logical that it should, for these articles were so beautiful and noteworthy that when they were handed down from generation to generation their beauty was appreciated by the various owners long before their value as antiques was recognized. They were designated as "Grandmother Schuyler's bureau" or the Governor Oliver Wolcott sideboard and were carefully preserved. Practically every experience of the collector of truly fine American antiques belies the popularly held conception of broken-down, dilapidated relics of the past. The condition of these pieces after many generations of successive owners is understandably remarkable. First, the wood selected was of the finest, naturally dried variety and did not warp or change its shape through the years. The various parts were so carefully joined with mortice and tenon and dovetails that glue was almost unnecessary. When veneer was used, it was fifty to one hundred times as thick as modern veneer, so that it did not have the same tendency to blister and crack. Each piece was built to last, like the pyramids, and that is the way they have survived.

Remember that I am speaking of the fine pieces made in the great centers of the Colonies by the best craftsmen the wealth of the cities attracted. Naturally, outside of the cities and large towns, not as much care could be taken in the fashioning of furniture and there were often severe limitations in the selection of wood available and in gifted craftsmen to construct it. Even in the cities, the same limitations applied to the poorer inhabitants. Certainly, the majority of the furniture made in the Colonies falls into the latter category —mediocre or inferior in design and construction. Even though the percentage of destruction of this type of furniture is higher than that of the classics, much has survived to be glamorized and romanticized, and its general decrepit condition is excused and even glorified because of its age. Such condition resulted from these factors: the furniture was not made of carefully selected and seasoned woods and tended to warp and break; it was not carefully constructed or joined; it was often poorly designed and later generations felt the need to improve on the defects. (This is very evident, for example, on chairs and sofas of all kinds, whose backs were made too straight to be comfortable; the tendency was to cut the back legs to create a greater tilt.) In general, later generations did not treasure it or carefully preserve it, so that it fell into neglect and abuse. Much of the furniture that found its way into chicken coops and attics *belonged there.*

Obviously, fine American antiques are expensive just as are fine furs, fine jewels, or fine homes. It is true that many people who love fine antiques cannot afford them. But this does not mean they should not know what is fine, because, in the last analysis, the ability to appreciate things of beauty is far more satisfying than the ability to possess them. Many people collect mediocrities in antiques and pay as much or more than they would for fine items. They would not do this if they realized that the things they are collecting are highly overrated.

The purpose of this book is to separate the wheat from the chaff among the more important schools of seventeenth and eighteenth century American furniture. This is done by comparison of examples similar in type but varying greatly in excellence of design and craftsmanship. It should be borne in mind that the difference in value between items in the "Good" and the "Best" columns is usually vast—the superior example being worth five, ten, or more times that of the inferior example of the same type. It is not feasible to place values on the various pieces under discussion, but this much can be said—those pieces listed in the "Best" column are usually worth over a thousand dollars, with the possible exception of only a few lesser types such as a simple mirror, occasional table, or single side chair. Even with these smaller items, the value of under one thousand dollars is the exception—some of the best single side chairs illustrated in this book are worth several thousand dollars apiece. Certain of the great masterpieces illustrated, notably from the Newport school or the Philadelphia school, are worth from ten to fifty thousand dollars or upward. It has been my father's experience throughout his forty-seven years of dealing in Early American antiques and my seventeen-year experience in the same field that these masterpieces seek their own level and that the quest for them at bargain prices is an illusion. More often than not, the neophyte collector is dismayed by the premium prices which certain of the items in the "Best" column have fetched and purchases similar examples of the "Good" or "Better" quality, believing them to be of the same value as their more illustrious cousins. If this book convinces the reader that the value of any piece of antique furniture is in direct ratio to its merit and its relative standing among contemporary examples of a similar type, it will have served its purpose.

Of course there are many more gradations of quality than the three (Good, Better, Best) used in this book, therefore each must cover a wide range. "Good" refers to examples from the worst to the mediocre, or average. "Better" refers to items by good or fine craftsmen but with a definite weakness either in proportion, design, or workmanship. The "Best" category is self-explanatory. However, because an item is listed in this column, it does not necessarily mean it is the most valuable specimen of its type, since another example of equal quality might contain more important detail or be a rare successful variation from the conventional. It does mean that it was made by a superior craftsman and that it is worthy of the most discriminating collection, assuming that it is well preserved.

The last chapter in the book attempts to classify the various stages of preservation in which American antique furniture is found and to evaluate the effect of various restorations which may occur.

ILLUSTRATIONS

GOOD

Pilgrim slat-back side chair, New England, circa 1680-1720. Fashioned by a carpenter who would have liked to turn out the chair shown at right, but failed to make the grade. The turnings of the legs, stretchers and stiles are not well defined and are ineptly done compared with the corresponding turnings on the other chair. Also by comparison, the finials are shapeless blobs.

BEST

Pilgrim slat-back side chair with the old black paint and original rush seat, New England, circa 1680-1720. Note the masterful turnings, the well-shaped finials and the vastly superior proportions (as compared with chair at left) of this fine Pilgrim chair.

BEST

Pilgrim white oak wainscot chair, made by Thomas Dennis, Ipswich, Mass., circa 1660-1700. While still closely influenced by the style then prevailing in the mother country, Dennis developed his own individualistic design, which, together with the distinctive American white quartered oak which differs from the English, makes the accent of this chair and the more elaborate one shown below definitely American.

BEST

Pilgrim white oak wainscot chair, made by Thomas Dennis, Ipswich, Mass., circa 1660-1700. This masterpiece, now in the Essex Institute, was long considered to be of English origin until the magazine **Antiques** published a series of articles illustrating several known wainscot chairs and a number of carved chests, all of which can definitely be traced to the shop of this great Pilgrim carver and joiner. The "New" in New England was already beginning to be asserted.

GOOD

Pilgrim Carver chair, New England, circa 1670-1700. An average chair with undistinguished turned back posts, finials and spindles.

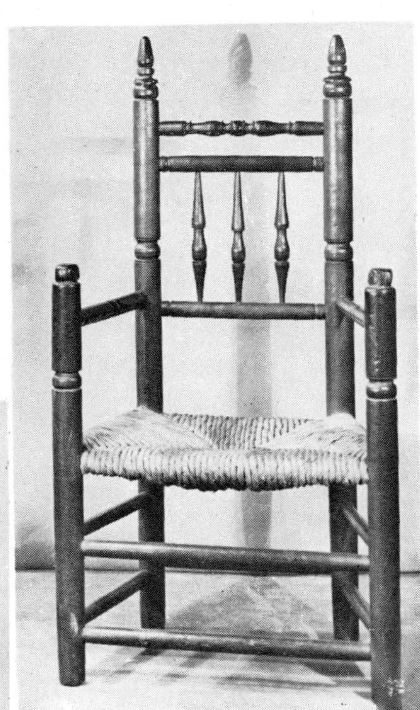

BETTER

Pilgrim Carver chair, New England, circa 1670-1700. A chair of considerable merit. Note the desirable bolder effect achieved by the thick back posts, the better turned finials and spindles as compared with those of the chair illustrated at right above.

BEST

Pilgrim Brewster chair, New England, circa 1670-1700. A great Pilgrim chair with vigorous heavy posts and magnificently turned finials and spindles.

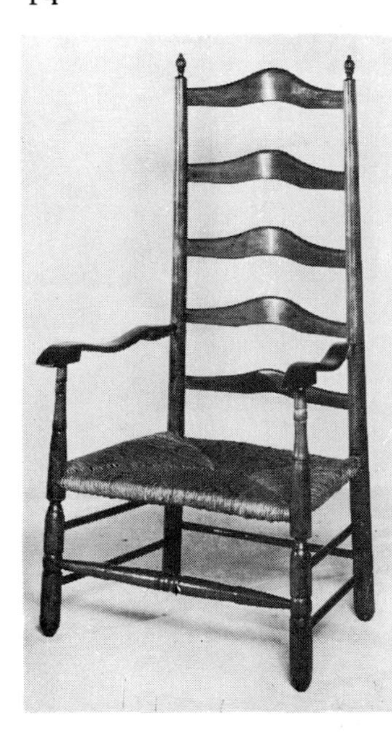

GOOD

Early slat-back armchair, Pennsylvania, circa 1680-1720. A weak chair with slender, poorly turned posts and front legs. The seat is too low and the back too high for perfect proportion.

BETTER

Early slat-back armchair, Pennsylvania, circa 1680-1720. This chair has better turnings than the example illustrated at left above, but the proportions are also inept. The back is too low and the chair appears too wide and squatty.

BEST

Early slat-back armchair, Pennsylvania, circa 1680-1720. An exceptional chair of fine proportions and with choice turnings. The well-modeled trumpet feet add rarity to an outstanding chair.

BEST

Pilgrim slat-back armchair, New England, circa 1680-1720. One of the great classics of the Pilgrim era. It epitomizes the strength and the dignity of the Pilgrim character in its heavy posts and its vigorous turnings. The shaping of the top slat is exceptionally fine.

GOOD

Pilgrim banister-back armchair, New England, circa 1680-1720. Weak turnings and unexciting proportions.

BETTER

Pilgrim banister-back armchair, New England, circa 1680-1720. A finer chair than the one shown at left above, with good turnings and more sophisticated lines.

BEST

Pilgrim banister-back armchair, New England, circa 1680-1720. Superlative chair with boldly turned stretcher which would excite any collector of early furniture. The finely carved crest, the excellently shaped arms and the superior outline of the banisters all help to place this chair in the highest category of rarity and desirability.

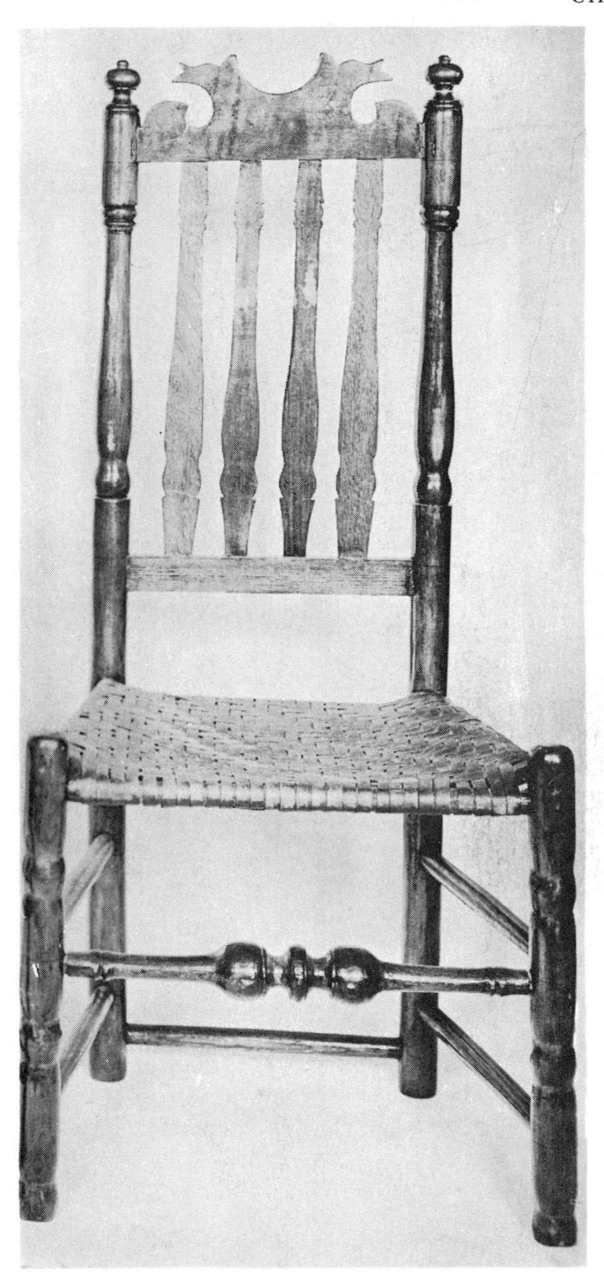

GOOD

Pilgrim banister-back side chair with shaped crest, New England, circa 1680-1720. A chair of above-average quality but of distinctly lesser stature than the superb chair shown at right. Not only does not have the slenderness and height, which gives the other chair such dignity, but the turnings of the back posts, legs and stretchers, as well as the split banisters, are of poorer quality.

BEST

Pilgrim banister-back side chair with Prince of Wales crest, New England, circa 1680-1720. A highly desirable chair of superb proportions and masterful turnings. Far more important than similar armchairs of lesser quality.

GOOD

Pilgrim side chair, New England, circa 1710-1730. A mediocre chair. The Spanish feet are not well formed; the serpentine crest rail and the turned stretcher are not first quality.

Two transitional Queen Anne side chairs, New England, circa 1710-1730. Side view of two almost identical chairs—except that one craftsman shaped a subtle curve in the back and the other took the path of least resistance, resulting in the stiff chair at the right.

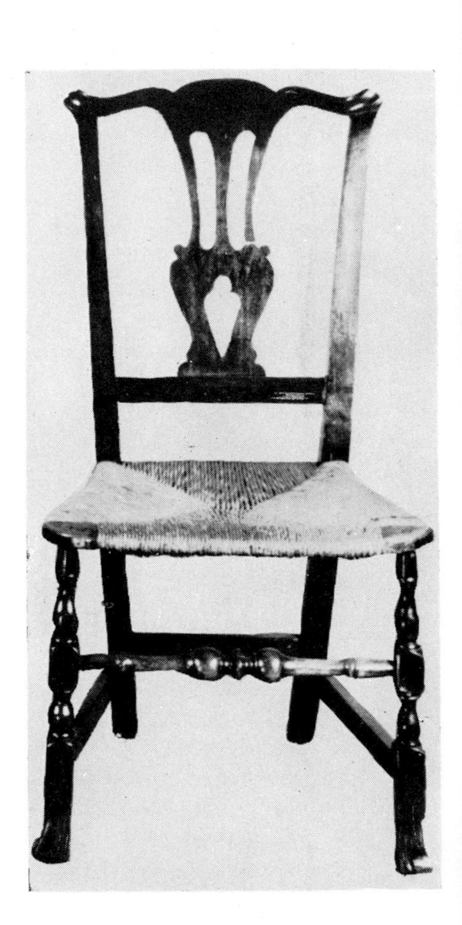

BEST

Pilgrim side chair, New England, circa 1710-1730. A lovely chair of excellent quality. The crest rail and Spanish feet are better formed than those of the example shown at top of page.

BEST

Transitional Queen Anne armchair, by John Gaines, Portsmouth, N. H., circa 1710-1730. The individualistic carved crest rail identifies this maker. A great masterpiece of pure Colonial design. Note the magnificent sweep of the highly prized ram's horn arms which are found only on a few of the finest examples of this period. Compare the superb modeling of the Spanish feet with the average treatment of the examples illustrated on page 18. No price is too great for a chair of this quality. It is now in a private collection.

BEST

Early Queen Anne armchair with cabriole legs and solid splat, Pennsylvania, circa 1720-1730. One of the great masterpieces of Pennsylvania early furniture. Note the magnificent, vigorous turned stretcher and the many effective refinements such as the scalloped apron and the chamfered edges of the cabriole legs. The proportions are excellent.

Side view of chair. The lines and detail are as impressive from this angle as from the front. The scalloped skirt on the side is exceptionally beautiful as is the shape of the horizontal arm with its knuckle terminal. Note the subtle serpentine sweep to the back post which adds to the comfort of the chair as well as to the line.

GOOD

Queen Anne walnut side chair with turned stretchers and straight front seat, New England, circa 1740-1760. An inferior chair with a shapeless splat and weak cabriole legs.

BETTER

Queen Anne walnut side chair with turned stretchers and straight front seat, New England, circa 1740-1760. A better chair than the one shown above, with a fine splat and scalloped apron; it suffers, however, from a heavy leg that appears to be swollen at the knees.

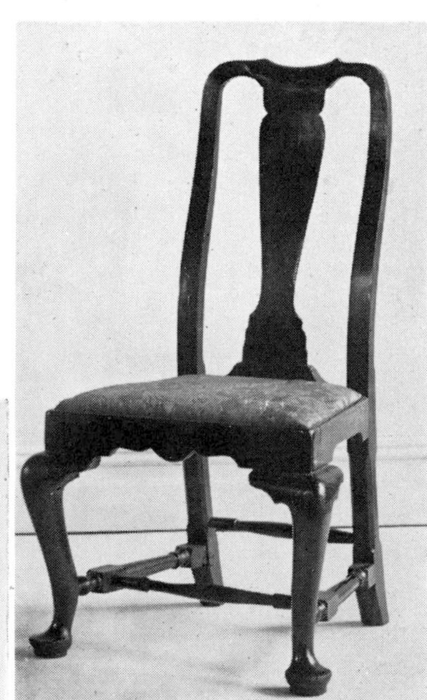

BEST

Queen Anne walnut side chair with turned stretchers and straight front seat, New England, circa 1740-1760. A beautifully modeled chair of excellent line and graceful cabriole leg.

BEST

Queen Anne walnut side chair, New England, circa 1740-1760. The rare vase-shaped splat and the general excellence of the chair make this a highly prized example. One of a set of four in a private collection.

BEST

Queen Anne walnut side chair with elongated shell in crest and shaped stiles, Rhode Island, circa 1740-1760. This type of shell is a very effective device; it is found mainly on Rhode Island chairs. The chair is excellent from all standpoints; the well-formed cabriole legs and the shaped stiles are more often found on fine Philadelphia chairs of the period.

BEST

Pair of Queen Anne walnut side chairs, Rhode Island, circa 1740-1760. This pair of chairs is of the utmost importance. Each has about every desirable feature one could possibly look for in a chair of this period—the fine shell, the vase-shaped splat, the shaped stiles, the finely carved knees and the claw and ball feet all successfully blended by an expert craftsman. The fact that these obviously Queen Anne chairs have claw and ball feet, which to some people automatically makes them Chippendale, shows the stiffness of our terminology. It makes little difference whether they are called Queen Anne, Chippendale or transitional; they rank among the best chairs of that era.

BEST

Queen Anne maple armchair, New England, circa 1720-1750. A choice example of a very scarce type, with finely shaped arms and arm supports. Few specimens have survived intact, and original examples such as this are much sought after.

GOOD

Queen Anne side chair with serpentine crest rail, Pennsylvania, circa 1740-1760. An inferior chair of skimpy proportions. The cabriole legs do not have sufficient height or well-defined curves.

BETTER

Queen Anne side chair with serpentine crest rail, Pennsylvania, circa 1740-1760. A better than average Queen Anne chair whose over-all proportions, as well as the treatment of the splat and crest rail, are far superior to those of the chair shown at left above.

BEST

Queen Anne side chair with serpentine crest rail, Pennsylvania, circa 1740-1760. Superior chair of Queen Anne type, with a beautiful scalloped apron and well-formed cabriole legs.

GOOD

Queen Anne side chair with balloon seat and back, Philadelphia, circa 1740-1760. An inferior chair by an ungifted craftsman who reached out of his class. It lacks the stature of best chair of this group, and the stiff lines of the cabriole legs fall short of achieving the effect desired in furniture of the Queen Anne period—that of a combination of curved members blended to form a harmonious unit.

BETTER

Queen Anne side chair with balloon seat and back, Philadelphia, circa 1740-1760. A better chair than the one at right above, with an excellent crest and splat. The cabriole legs and drake feet suffer by comparison with example shown below, as does the carving on the knees.

BEST

Queen Anne side chair with balloon seat and back, Philadelphia, circa 1740-1760. The perfection of line and noble stature of this chair epitomize the essential greatness of our Colonial craftsmen—their ability to achieve beauty in simplicity. Note the superior curve to the cabriole leg, the finely modeled drake foot and the depth and crispness of the carved shell and pendant on the knee. The magnificently figured splat had to be shaped from a mahogany log at least four inches thick, as the splat has a decided scoop which this photograph does not depict. The fine crest expertly completes the curve of the stiles.

BEST

Queen Anne side chair, Philadelphia, circa 1750-1760. A superlative chair with vigorous carving and a masterful splat. Note how each of the scrolls on the crest flows into the next.

BEST

Queen Anne side chairs, Philadelphia, circa 1750-1760. These chairs represent the richest development of this type of chair. They were expensive when made for a prominent Philadelphia family two hundred years ago, and proved to be a wise investment. Not only have they been enjoyed by several generations of descendants but today each well-preserved example is worth several thousands of dollars. Note the effectiveness of the concave seat frame with the carved shell, also the bold scrolls in the crest rail.

GOOD

Queen Anne armchair, Philadelphia, circa 1740-1760. A stiff specimen with many crudities such as the splat and the apron. Compare the arm supports of this chair with those of the two other chairs shown on this page.

BEST

Queen Anne armchair, Philadelphia, circa 1740-1760. A very fine chair with the superior balloon back and seat. Note the expert modeling of the horizontal arm—the scooped section relieves the chunky effect present on chairs without this feature. The scrolled terminals provide a feeling of strength. The effective blending of the many curved members of a chair of this type is noteworthy.

BEST

Queen Anne armchair, Philadelphia, circa 1740-1760. An American classic, certainly one of the finest of the Philadelphia armchairs. It boasts a superbly carved unique crest rail and well-modeled drake feet. The turned stretchers are seldom found on this type chair.

BETTER

Chippendale armchair with pierced splat, Philadelphia, circa 1750-1780. A pleasing chair of average quality. The design of the splat is undoubtedly derived from the same model as was used for chair shown below, but the superiority of the latter is striking. The crest rail of this example is relatively crude. The arms and arm supports are of above-average finesse.

BEST

Chippendale armchair with pierced splat, Philadelphia, circa 1750-1780. A choice chair, superior in workmanship and design—evidenced in the crest rail, the arms and arm supports and the more desirable cabriole legs.

BETTER

Early Chippendale armchair, Philadelphia, circa 1740-1760. Both this example and the chair shown below have claw and ball feet and solid splats in common, but there the similarity ends. The arms and arm supports of this chair are chunky and crudely formed; its lines are straight and angular compared with the flowing curves of the other chair.

BEST

Queen Anne armchair, Philadelphia, circa 1740-1760. A superb chair of perfect symmetry. Many would call this priceless chair Chippendale because of the claw and ball feet. If the same chair, with its balloon seat and back, had drake feet it would be called Queen Anne. Such a controversy proves only that there is no sharp dividing line between the periods in the eighteenth century. These periods merely aid in placing pieces in general categories. Isn't it more important that the chair itself be a masterpiece, rather than whether it be Queen Anne or Chippendale?

GOOD

Chippendale armchair, Philadelphia, circa 1750-1780. A mediocre chair with a weak splat and crude arm supports.

BEST

Chippendale armchair, Philadelphia, circa 1750-1780. A choice Philadelphia armchair of fine line and expert workmanship. Note the harmonious blending of all members and the sturdy, masculine quality which the chair imparts. The interlaced splat is of more conventional design than that of the chair shown above, but it is far more desirable because it is successfully executed. Armchairs of this quality are rare and valuable, as few have survived intact.

BEST

Chippendale armchair, Philadelphia, circa 1750-1780. This chair, while of the same quality as the chair shown below, suffers from a deep apron which, due to modern sanitary developments, no longer has the function it had in the eighteenth century.

BETTER

Chippendale armchair, Philadelphia, circa 1750-1780. Very few Philadelphia armchairs of this fine quality have survived intact.

GOOD

Chippendale armchair with pierced splat, Philadelphia circa 1750-1780. The weakest of the three chairs illustrated on this page. The perfectly straight apron offends the eye, and the pierced splat is undistiguished.

BETTER

Chippendale armchair with pierced splat, Philadelphia, circa 1750-1780. A better chair, with exceptionally fine arms and arm supports. It suffers, however, from a cumbersome apron which the craftsman tried unsuccessfully to relieve by scrolling.

BEST

Chippendale armchair with pierced splat, Philadelphia, circa 1750-1780. A very fine armchair, with the best proportions and superbly carved knees. The difference in quality between this pierced splat and the one on the chair shown at top left is striking, for they are almost identical in general form.

GOOD

Chippendale side chair, Philadelphia, circa 1750-1770. An average chair of too delicate proportions. The most desirable characteristics for a chair of this type are strength and boldness. These qualities are successfully achieved in the example shown below.

BEST

Chippendale side chair, Philadelphia, circa 1750-1770. A "masculine" chair which successfully combines strength with symmetry. The relationship of the shell and scrolls in the crest to the earlier balloon-back chairs is apparent.

BETTER

Chippendale mahogany side chair, Philadelphia, circa 1750-1780. For some inexplicable reason this craftsman left the bottom portion of the splat solid. The resulting incompleteness is evident when compared with the chair shown below. Note how the ankle of this chair sags where it meets the claw and ball foot.

BEST

Chippendale mahogany side chair, Philadelphia, circa 1750-1780. A choice chair of fine proportion and beauty of detail.

BEST

Chippendale mahogany side chair, Philadelphia, circa 1750-1780. This chair ranks among the finest chairs of the Philadelphia group because of its perfection of line and superior craftsmanship. Note the depth of the well-placed, restrained carving.

BEST

Chippendale mahogany side chair, Philadelphia, circa 1750-1780. A Philadelphia masterpiece. Note the masterful treatment of the crest and the superb quality of the carving. Those few Chippendale chairs which successfully combine fine proportions with highest quality carving, such as this example, are understandably valuable.

BEST

Chippendale curly maple side chair, Philadelphia, circa 1750-1780. One of the masterpieces fashioned from native curly maple, a very hard wood to work with. Few examples as sophisticated as this were fashioned from it.

BEST

Right. Chippendale mahogany side chair, Philadelphia, circa 1750-1780. One of a set of chairs that belonged to George Washington and stood in the presidential mansion in Philadelphia. It is well worthy of its illustrious background, representing the highest development of the Philadelphia Chippendale school. The crest rail is a masterpiece in itself, with the bold scroll ears, the carved tassel and cord and the fine center motif. The finely carved convex shell in the center of the seat frame is very effective.

GOOD

Chippendale mahogany side chair, Philadelphia, circa 1750-1780. The least successful of this type, with a straight uninteresting crest rail. The cabriole legs do not have as fine a curve as those of the Randolph chair, illustrated on page 37.

BETTER

Chippendale mahogany side chair, Philadelphia, circa 1750-1780. This chair, even without carving, most closely follows the pattern of the Randolph chair. However, the chair presents an elongated appearance and the back is too high for perfect symmetry.

BETTER

Chippendale mahogany side chair, Philadelphia, circa 1750-1780. A fine chair that approaches the Randolph chair in excellence but does not reach it in execution or quality of carving. The cabriole legs and claw and ball feet are not as well fashioned. The scrolled apron is unusual and effective.

BEST

Chippendale mahogany side chair, bearing the label of Benjamin Randolph, Philadelphia, circa 1760-1775. The ultimate of this type and one of the greatest of the Philadelphia chairs. The carving on the triple-arched crest rail and on the knees is first quality. The cabriole legs achieve a perfect curve and the claw and ball feet are well formed. On the basis of this labeled chair in the Karolik Collection, most of the chairs with this type splat are attributed to Randolph—many of them erroneously. Courtesy of Museum of Fine Arts, Boston, M. & M. Karolik Collection.

Close-up of back of labeled Randolph chair. It is no wonder that other Philadelphia craftsmen adopted this beautiful design, but none of the examples shown on page 36 achieves the magnificence of this example.

BETTER

Chippendale mahogany side chair, Philadelphia, circa 1750-1780. Attributed to James Gillingham on the basis of the distinctive, carved crest rail found on a few labeled examples by this maker. A fine chair with an elaborate and somewhat heavy splat.

BEST

Chippendale mahogany side chair, Philadelphia, circa 1750-1780. Attributed to James Gillingham. A superlative chair, which alone places Gillingham among the foremost Philadelphia cabinetmakers. His chairs are usually more delicate and refined than examples by other makers, yet they retain the vigorous quality necessary for success in a chair of this period. Note the raised molded edges of the splat, the typical crest rail with the carved scroll ears, the carved center ornament in the arched seat frame, the slender cabriole legs and small claw and ball feet—all favorite devices of this master craftsman. The incised pattern on the stiles is rare.

BEST

Chippendale mahogany side chair with solid splat, Philadelphia, circa 1750-1780. A chair of the finest quality and proportions. The carved shells on the ears are a rare variation.

BEST

Chippendale mahogany side chair, Philadelphia, circa 1750-1780. A bold masterful chair that belonged to the famous Revolutionary General "Mad" Anthony Wayne. Observe the fluted stiles and the excellent crest rail. The design of the splat is unusual and successful.

BEST

Chippendale mahogany side chair, Philadelphia, circa 1750-1780. A superlative chair with architectural perfection and original design. The curve of the cabriole leg and the excellence of the claw and ball foot are of a caliber which most Philadelphia craftsmen aimed at but few achieved.

BEST

Chippendale mahogany tassel-back side chair, Philadelphia, circa 1750-1780. The ultimate in achievement in a Philadelphia chair from every standpoint. The proportions are stately and the design of the splat is brilliant. With all its richness the chair is not overdone. The carving is of the highest quality and none of it is superfluous to the design. Note the stop-fluted stiles. Courtesy of Museum of Fine Arts, Boston, M. & M. Karolik Collection.

GOOD

Chippendale armchair with pierced splat, Philadelphia, circa 1750-1780. An average armchair with a pleasing arm but with a ponderous apron and a weak splat.

BEST

Chippendale mahogany side chair with pierced splat, Philadelphia, circa 1750-1780. A choice side chair which, because of its excellence, is worth considerably more than the armchair shown above. Note the finely pierced splat with the effective scrolls, the expert curve to the cabriole legs and the finely modeled claw and ball feet.

GOOD

Chippendale mahogany side chair, New York, circa 1750-1780. Obviously derived from the chair illustrated below, but, stripped of its carving, it has become weak and uninspiring. I have rarely seen a chair, originally designed as a carved type, which is successful when the carving is eliminated.

BEST

Chippendale mahogany tassel-back side chair, New York, circa 1750-1780. Several sets of this effective pattern with slight variations were made for various branches of the important Van Renssalaer family. A choice New York chair of brilliant design and well-placed carving. The distinctive crest rail and the gadroon molding are conventional for this type chair. The cabriole leg is of typical New York form—the section between the knee and the claw and ball foot has a less sweeping curve than on the Philadelphia variety.

GOOD

Chippendale mahogany side chair with diamond-shaped splat, New York, circa 1750-1780. A crude, clumsy and poorly executed example. This is not because of the overstuffed upholstered seat, which can be corrected, but is rather because of the poorly formed cabriole legs, the inept claw and ball feet and the amateurish splat and crest rail.

BETTER

Chippendale mahogany side chair with diamond-shaped splat, New York, circa 1750-1780. A better example than the one shown at left, with finely carved knees and crest rail.

BEST

Chippendale mahogany side chair with diamond-shaped splat, New York, circa 1750-1780. One of a set made for Edmund Johnson. A superlative chair with rounded seat frame, unsurpassed among examples of New York chairs. Note the brilliant blending of the curves of the apron, seat frame and cabriole legs. The carved crest rail far surpasses those of the two other chairs shown on this page, in line as well as in craftsmanship.

BETTER

Chippendale mahogany side chair, Salem, Mass., circa 1750-1780. A fine chair of slightly heavy proportions, especially evident in the splat.

BEST

Chippendale mahogany side chair, Salem, Mass., circa 1750-1780. A typical chair of high caliber that shows the prevalent tendency in Salem and Boston to retain the turned stretchers which were so popular during the earlier Queen Anne period.

BEST

Chippendale mahogany side chair, Salem, Mass., circa 1750-1780. A beautifully proportioned chair. The perfect curve of the cabriole leg and the superb claw and ball foot are worth considerable attention.

BETTER

Chippendale mahogany side chair, Salem, Mass., circa 1750-1780. A remarkable study in contrast, for both chairs shown on this page were made in the same shop and are identical except that in this chair the carving has been eliminated from the back. Certainly the carved chair is the more successful—the maker of this chair would have done better to have used a pattern which lent itself to simplicity if this was the effect he was attempting to achieve.

BEST

Chippendale mahogany side chair, Salem, Mass., circa 1750-1780. One of a pair of chairs in a private collection and from the same set as a pair in the Metropolitan Museum. The beauty and bold original design of these chairs are admirable. Note the typical Salem cabriole leg and claw and ball foot—the two flanking claws grasping the ball of each foot are swept back more than on chairs of other localities.

GOOD

Chippendale mahogany side chair with straight legs and stretchers, Philadelphia, circa 1750-1780. A chair of uninspired design with a heavy solid splat.

BEST

Chippendale mahogany side chair with straight legs and stretchers, Philadelphia, circa 1750-1780. A fine chair with excellent splat and crest rail. Note how the vertical members of the splat flow into the crest with no break in unity.

GOOD

Chippendale mahogany ladder-back side chair, New England, circa 1750-1780. A chair of mediocre quality. It is narrow and skimpy; the pierced slats are not as finely formed as those in the chairs shown below.

BETTER

Chippendale mahogany ladder-back side chair, New England, circa 1750-1780. A typical chair of excellent quality. The pierced horizontal slats are well executed and the chair exhibits balanced proportion.

BEST

Chippendale mahogany ladder-back side chair, New England, circa 1750-1780. An American classic. Note the subtle serpentine curves of the slats and the molded edges as well as the superbly carved centers. The saddle seat adds to the fluency of the design and also serves to provide additional comfort.

BEST

Chippendale mahogany armchair, Newburyport, Mass., circa 1750-1780. A choice and rare armchair by Joseph Short, a well-known Newburyport cabinetmaker. The distinctive arm supports with the flaring base occur in several labeled chairs by this maker. The proportions create a feeling of strength and vigor which probably reflected the character of its original owner.

BEST

Chippendale mahogany ladder-back side chair, Philadelphia, circa 1750-1780. A typical example of a fine Philadelphia chair. Dozens of similar sets of this pattern were made in and around Philadelphia. The rounded contours where the back posts meet the crest and the typical serpentine crest with its molded edge vary but little in the many examples in existence. The chief differences occur in the seat fronts, which are sometimes straight and sometimes serpentine—also in the legs which are either molded or have a beaded edge.

BEST

Chippendale mahogany ladder-back side chair, Philadelphia, circa 1750-1780. An important original design attributed to Trotter of Philadelphia on the basis of a signed sketch by this maker still in existence. Few chairs of this brilliant design have survived, and these are highly prized by collectors. They have in common the double arched slats with the carved motif in the center and the carved medallions in the corners. The effective spiral beading in each of the molded legs of this chair adds to its importance.

GOOD

Hepplewhite shield-back armchair, New York, circa 1780. This cramped provincial armchair is an enlightening example of the variance in quality (see below) possible in chairs derived from the same basic design.

BEST

Hepplewhite mahogany shield-back armchair, New York, circa 1780. An American classic. The superb proportions and the inspired design of the splat form a symphony.

BEST

Left. Hepplewhite mahogany shield-back side chair, New York, circa 1780. One of the most noteworthy of the justifiably famous New York Hepplewhite school. The folds of the drapery fall so naturally they seem almost real. The shield-shaped back with its bold serpentine crest and pointed base is a separate unit, yet it blends with the rest of the chair to form a harmonious whole.

BEST

Right. Hepplewhite mahogany shield-back side chair, New York, circa 1780. A superlative chair, probably an early Duncan Phyfe creation. The stately proportions of the tall, slender shield-back are typical of New York design. The delicate reeded legs and spade feet are of the highest order.

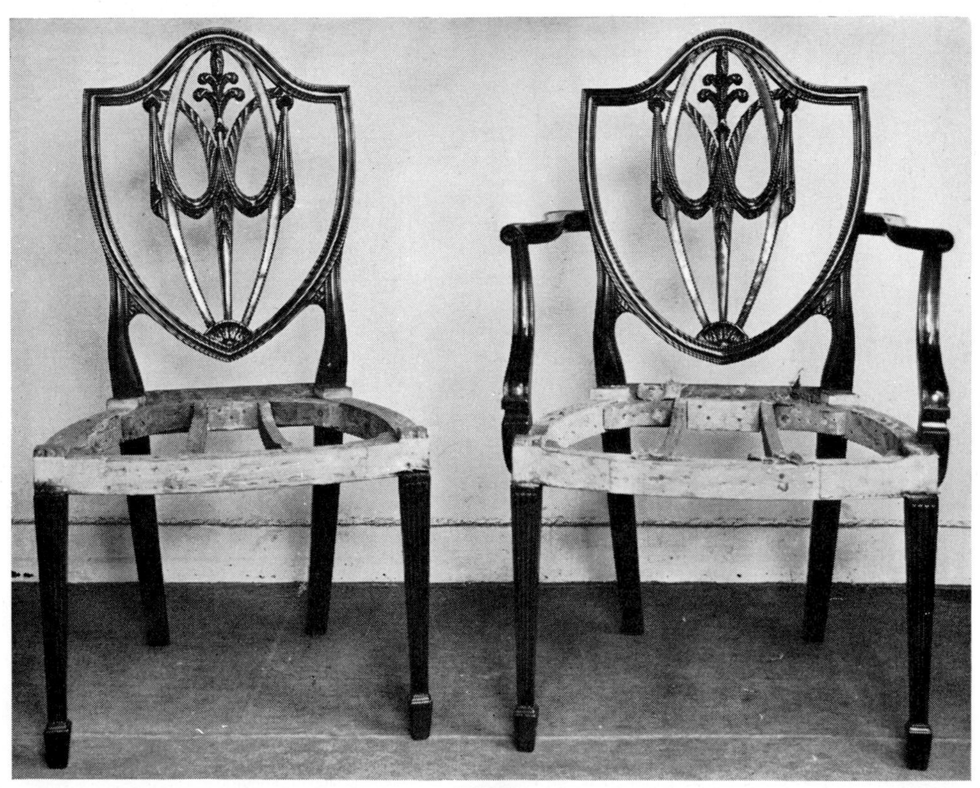

BEST

Hepplewhite armchair and side chair stripped of upholstery, New York, circa 1780. The horizontal cross braces dovetailed into the front and back members of the seat frames were used frequently in New York chairs and help to identify them.

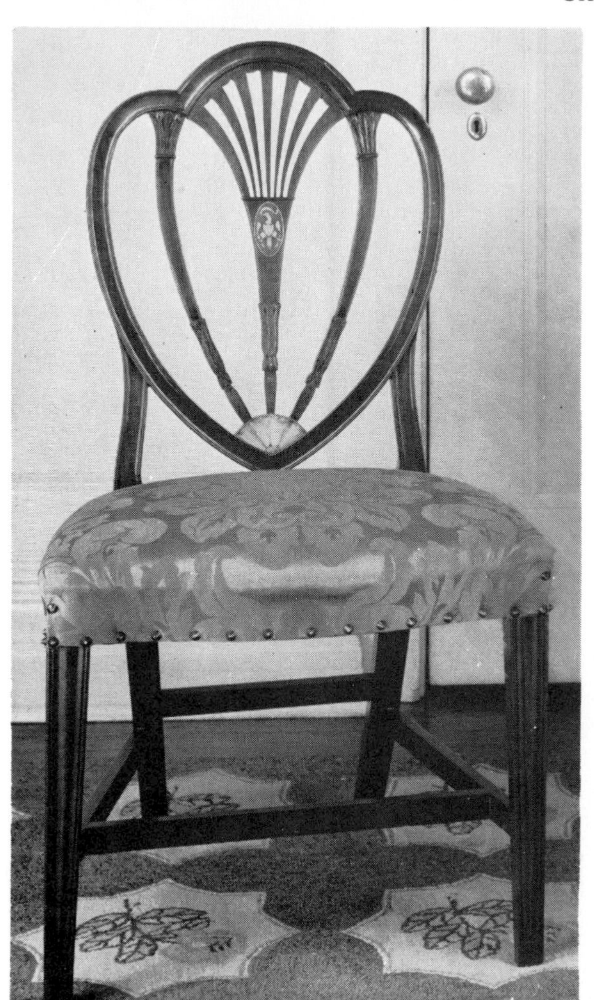

BEST

Hepplewhite mahogany side chair, Baltimore, Md., circa 1780. A chair of great importance, because of the inlaid eagle and shield, proud symbol of our newly acquired independence. The shield-shaped back is well designed and executed.

BEST

Hepplewhite mahogany side chair, Maryland, circa 1780. One of a set of chairs made for Charles Carroll of Carrollton—a signer of the Declaration of Independence—and well worthy of this distinguished citizen. Obviously, Charles Carroll commissioned the best craftsman in his locality to design and fashion an outstanding set of chairs regardless of price. The deep well-placed carving is first quality and the design is brilliant.

BETTER

Hepplewhite mahogany side chair with inlaid urn, Connecticut, circa 1780. A typical Connecticut chair of above-average quality. It did not reach the heights achieved by its illustrious Rhode Island contemporary examples.

BEST

Hepplewhite mahogany side chair, Newport, R. I., circa 1780. A truly superlative chair, in all probability made by John Goddard. The intricate and well-executed splat is a triumph of original Colonial design. The bold bulge of the stiles where they meet the crest is an effective device.

BEST

Hepplewhite side chair, by Samuel McIntire, Salem, Mass., circa 1780. The breadth and balance as well as the restraint of this creation represent the ultimate in the Hepplewhite era.

BEST

Hepplewhite side chair, signed by Stephen Badlam, carver, of Dorchester, Mass., circa 1780. This outstanding chair was carved and probably also designed by Stephen Badlam who, except for Samuel McIntire, was the best known carver of Boston or vicinity. His name is branded into the back of the seat rail. Note the saddle seat, unusual in this period, and the stop-fluting in the legs.

Back of Badlam chair. The splat is a brilliant piece of workmanship.

BEST

Hepplewhite mahogany side chair, made and signed by Benjamin Frothingham, of Charlestown, Mass., and carved by Samuel McIntire, of Salem, Mass., circa 1780. The importance of a signed chair of this quality cannot be overemphasized, since it proves the established practice of furniture being made by one craftsman and being sent to a master carver to be completed. Unquestionably this superlative chair was signed so that it would not be returned to the wrong shop after being carved. Benjamin Frothingham, cabinetmaker, was a major in the Revolutionary War and a close friend of Washington, who made a special visit to Charlestown to see his friend during the first year of his presidency. This is one of the best-documented pieces of Early American furniture.

Signature in seat frame of above chair.

Detail of back of Frothingham chair. It is easy to understand why McIntire had the reputation of being the best carver of his day. The crisp, delicate vines in the crest show the confident hand of a genius.

Sketch signed by Samuel McIntire, now in the Essex Institute. That the Frothingham chair is a direct outcome of this sketch can hardly be questioned.

Relatively crude carving on the crest rail of a mediocre Salem chair.

GOOD

Sheraton mahogany armchair, New York, circa 1800. This chair reminds one of an attempt by an ungifted grammar school student to paint the Mona Lisa. It would be greatly overpriced at one hundred dollars, while the chair shown below would be a great bargain at one thousand dollars.

BEST

Sheraton mahogany armchair, New York, circa 1800. The acme of perfection in design and execution. A notable chair of which several excellent sets were produced by New York cabinetmakers. The center carved splat contained within an arched area is well balanced and superbly carved. The reeded legs and full spade feet are most desirable features.

BEST

Sheraton mahogany armchair, New York, circa 1820. Choice chair of a pattern popular in New York. Several sets are known, all of uniformly high caliber. It should be noted that this type chair was copied fifty or seventy-five years ago by a New York cabinetmaker. The reproductions fooled some unwary buyers. The difference in proportion and quality from the original is apparent to the student.

BEST

Sheraton mahogany side chair, attributed to Samuel McIntire, Salem, Mass., circa 1800. An appealing chair, with the rare feature of a carved spread eagle in the center panel.

BEST

Sheraton mahogany side chair, Philadelphia, circa 1800. A fine chair carved by a master.

GOOD

Sheraton m a h o g a n y chair, New York, circa 1820. An ungainly, heavy chair with awkward legs and disjointed parts.

BETTER

Sheraton mahogany chair, New York, circa 1800-1810. A better quality chair, but far from outstanding. The reeded legs are more slender than in the above example and the cross splat is a higher development.

BEST

Sheraton mahogany chair, by Duncan Phyfe, New York, circa 1800. A fine chair of excellent proportions. The curved seat frame aids the fluency of the lines. The crest is carved with the typical Phyfe drapery. The chair exhibits the master's touch which the above examples lack.

GOOD

Late Sheraton side chair, New York, circa 1810-1820. An awkward chair of no particular merit.

BETTER

Late Sheraton side chair, New York, circa 1810-1820. A moderately pleasing chair.

BEST

Late Sheraton side chair, New York, circa 1810-1820. An exceptional chair with a beautifully carved spread eagle forming the center splat.

GOOD

Late Sheraton side chair with hairy paw feet, New York, circa 1810-1820. An undistinguished chair with somewhat abbreviated feet.

BETTER

Late Sheraton side chair with hairy paw feet, New York, circa 1810-1820. A rather heavy chair with an interesting but somewhat disjointed center splat.

BETTER

Late Sheraton side chair with hairy paw feet, New York, circa 1810-1820. A fine lyre-back chair by Duncan Phyfe. The turned reeded crest rail is not as successful as the paneled rectangular crest of the chair shown below.

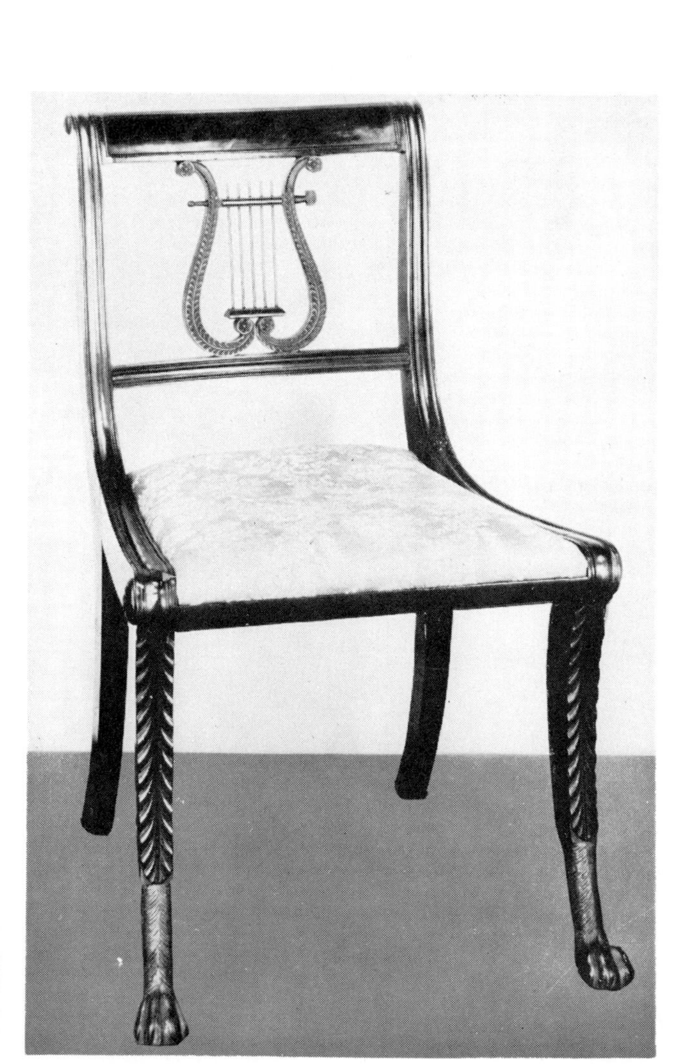

BEST

Late Sheraton side chair, by Duncan Phyfe, New York, circa 1810-1820. One of a set made for Arthur Middleton, signer of the Declaration of Independence, it is a masterpiece in its own right. The legs have perfect stature—the acanthus and hairy paw carving is superb as is the distinctive carving of the lyre splat.

GOOD

Sheraton mahogany armchair, New York, circa 1820. A grotesque specimen by a craftsman of great ambition but of unfortunate limitations.

BETTER

Sheraton mahogany armchair, New York, circa 1800-1810. An above-average chair except for its undistinguished splat. The serpentine reeded arms and the reeded legs and seat frame are details employed by Duncan Phyfe. The chair was made either in his workshop or by a contemporary New York craftsman. Whether or not it was made by Phyfe, it is not as valuable as the chair shown below because it is not as slender or as well modeled.

BEST

Sheraton mahogany armchair, by Duncan Phyfe, New York, circa 1800-1810. A superlative Phyfe armchair. Note the serpentine curve of the arms and the effective double cross splats. The carving is done in keeping with Phyfe's usual high standards.

BEST

Queen Anne walnut wing chair, New England, circa 1720-1750. A choice representative wing chair of a type which graced many fine Colonial homes. This chair has since been stripped of its Victorian covering and properly upholstered.

The chair at top left, in the frame

BEST

Queen Anne walnut wing chair, New England, circa 1720-1750. A fine representative example of this much sought after type.

BEST

Queen Anne mahogany wing chair, attributed to Job Townsend, Newport, R. I., circa 1750-1760. An outstanding and exceedingly rare chair of fine quality, with the flat stretchers and C scrolls in the legs. It is now in a private collection along with a matching set of side chairs.

BEST

Pilgrim "Spanish" foot maple wing chair, New England, 1700-1720. A superlative example, one of the best of the few such chairs which have survived. Note the boldly turned center stretcher, the height and fluency of the back, the excellent proportions of the chair as a whole. The dignity of this chair is understandable, for it was handed down in the family of Theophilus Parsons, the first Chief Justice of the Massachusetts Supreme Court. It is difficult for some people to visualize how a wing chair will look when upholstered. The illustrations below are of a chair stripped and upholstered.

BEST

Queen Anne walnut wing chair, New England, circa 1720-1750. A magnificent chair properly upholstered in fine crewelwork. No collector demands or desires the original upholstery on an antique wing chair or sofa, but he does require the original framework.

View of the center chair stripped to the frame. The substantial construction, from thick beams of curly maple in the seat frame and the back legs extending to the crest hewn from one piece of rock maple, is the reason for the lasting qualities of these chairs.

BEST

Chippendale mahogany wing chair, Rhode Island, circa 1750-1780. A choice chair which admirably expresses the boldness and strength of character of our pre-Revolutionary Rhode Island citizenry.

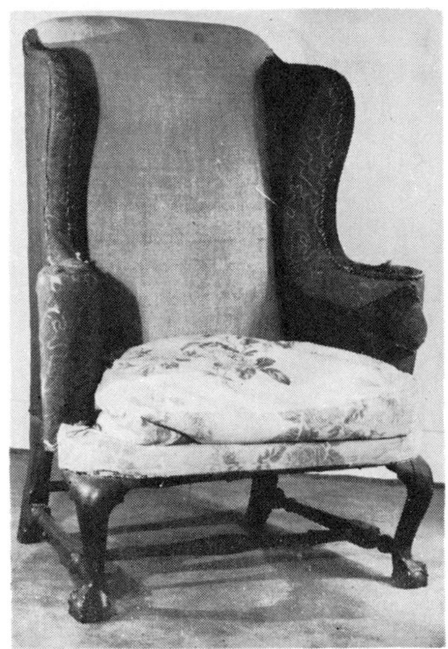

BEST

Queen Anne wing and slipper chairs with claw and ball feet, Rhode Island, circa 1740-1760. Each chair (shown at center and at bottom of page) is outstanding in its own right. Their rarity is greatly enhanced by being, to our knowledge, the only known chairs which have remained together as a pair through the many generations. The wing chair, as shown here, still retains the original blue moreen covering on the arms and wings.

GOOD

Chippendale wing chair with turned stretchers, New England, circa 1750-1780. A stiff, clumsy chair of angular lines which would prevent the best upholsterer in the world from making it graceful. The practically vertical back does not make for comfort. The better chairs of this period have an adequate tilt to the back.

BEST

Chippendale wing chair with turned stretchers, New England, circa 1750-1780. A fine chair of excellent proportions. The back has an adequate tilt and the wings blend with the curve of the crest, thereby avoiding the boxy appearance of the chair shown above.

BEST

Chippendale mahogany wing chair with roll arms, Philadelphia, circa 1750-1780. One of several wing chairs of this style produced in Philadelphia, it is certainly the highest development of an American Chippendale wing chair. The curved seat, the flaring roll arms and the shaped crest rail all aid in achieving the beauty of line of this chair.

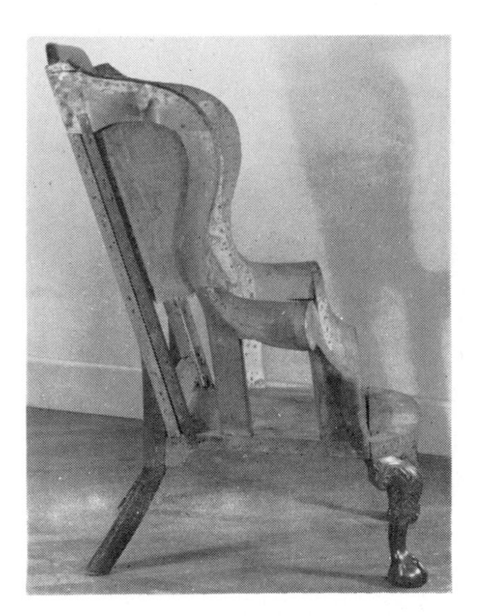

Side view of chair shown above. The bold rake of the back legs and the compensating slope of the back remind one of the proud stance of a thoroughbred race horse. Note the masterful shaping of the roll arms.

Front view of same chair in the frame. The superlative lines of this chair were properly followed by an expert upholsterer (Ernest LoNano), resulting in the incomparable chair shown at top of page.

GOOD

Chippendale mahogany wing chair with plain legs, New England, circa 1750-1780. This chair has the highly desirable serpentine wings and crest, but was made by a cabinetmaker with little feeling for proper proportion. It is obviously too wide and too squatty, making it an inferior chair.

BEST

Chippendale mahogany wing chair with molded legs, New England, circa 1750-1780. View in the frame. This chair, with the serpentine-shaped wings and bold serpentine crest, is one of the highest developments of this type.

BEST

Chippendale mahogany wing chair with molded legs, New England, circa 1750-1780. A choice chair of fine, stately proportions and subtle line.

GOOD

"Martha Washington" armchair, New England, circa 1760-1780. A crude country-made chair with shapeless arms.

BETTER

"Martha Washington" mahogany armchair, New England, circa 1760-1780. A better-made chair than the one shown above, but with short stumpy legs and broad seat which is heavy in relation to the top.

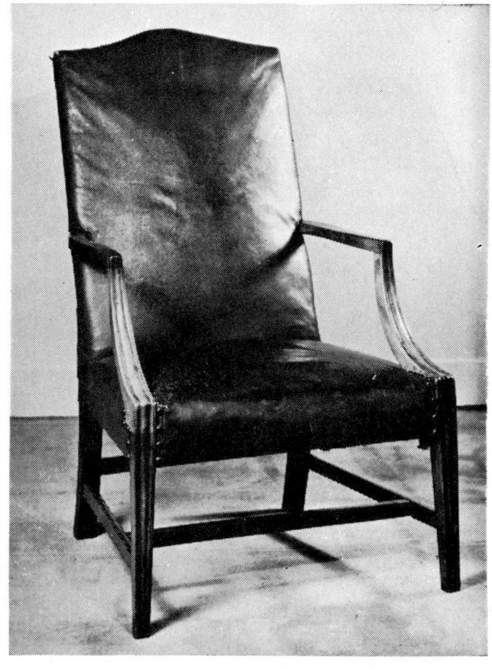

BEST

"Martha Washington" mahogany armchair, New England, circa 1760-1780. Beautifully proportioned armchair with finely molded legs and arm supports.

A view of the chair illustrated below as it was when first discovered, intact but with overstuffed upholstery. It illustrates how improper upholstery can spoil the lines of the finest chair.

BEST

Hepplewhite "Martha Washington" armchair with fluted legs, New England, circa 1780. A very fine chair, also important historically since it belonged to General Stark of Revolutionary fame. Note the finely scooped arms and the excellent serpentine crest.

BEST

Chippendale mahogany wing chair with Marlborough feet, Philadelphia, circa 1750-1780. This masterful and extremely rare chair more closely follows the low, broad English proportion than do the New England examples. The crest is shaped like the great Philadelphia sofas and the whole chair exudes strength and character. The Victorian covering on the chair detracts from its beauty and has probably been replaced with an appropriate silk damask.

BEST

"Martha Washington" armchair, New England, circa 1760-1780. An outstanding, well-balanced chair. The molding follows up the horizontal arm and terminates in a carved pinwheel. The broad part of the horizontal arm usually appeared heavy in most chairs of this style. This careful craftsman would not allow this. He scooped out the inner surface and placed a raised border on the outer edge, brilliantly overcoming a usually objectionable feature.

BEST

Hepplewhite "Martha Washington" mahogany inlaid armchair, New England, circa 1780. A stately chair of exceptional quality. The tall slender lines epitomize the proportion preferred by the Colonists against the broader proportion of the English contemporary examples. This chair has finely scooped arms and an unusually fine crest.

GOOD

Hepplewhite "Martha Washington" mahogany inlaid armchair, New England, circa 1780. A less desirable example than the one shown below, with a stiff straight back which detracts from the fluency of line as well as the comfort of the chair. From such chairs did the erroneous reputation of stiff and uncomfortable antique chairs develop.

BEST

Hepplewhite "Martha Washington" mahogany inlaid armchair, New England, circa 1780. A very fine chair with a nicely sloping back.

BEST

Sheraton "Martha Washington" mahogany armchair, Salem, circa 1800. An outstanding example. Few successful armchairs of this period have survived.

GOOD

Chippendale mahogany corner chair, Philadelphia, circa 1750-1780. An average chair with a cumbersome base.

BETTER

Queen Anne walnut corner chair, New England, circa 1720-1750. A well-executed chair with fine openwork splats and cushioned pad feet. Most of the chairs of this period had turned stretchers.

BEST

Chippendale mahogany corner chair, Salem, Mass., circa 1750-1780. A chair of outstanding quality and rarity. The carved cabriole legs and claw and ball foot are first quality, as are the openwork splats in the back. The fluted columns are exceptional.

BEST

Queen Anne walnut corner chair, New England, circa 1740-1760. One of the best New England corner chairs. The effectiveness of the four cabriole legs and the shaped front is apparent.

BEST

Chippendale mahogany corner chair, New York, circa 1750-1780. The ultimate in a corner chair. Note the superbly shaped arm supports similar to those used on the best Queen Anne armchairs. Courtesy of Museum of Fine Arts, Boston, M. & M. Karolik Collection.

GOOD

Windsor armchair with continuous arms, New England eighteenth century. Good from the seat up. The crude legs are a definite disappointment.

BETTER

Windsor armchair with continuous arms, New England, eighteenth century. Good except for the shapeless seat. Why the craftsman, who could produce these finely turned legs and the fine bow-back and arms, did not make a well-shaped seat is hard to understand. But because of the plank seat, the chair is of a lower order than the one shown below.

BEST

Windsor armchair with continuous arms, New England, eighteenth century. A perfect chair with the best turnings, a fine rake to the legs and arm supports, also a well-shaped seat.

GOOD

Left. Windsor armchair with mahogany arms, Rhode Island, eighteenth century. Straight angular chair with uninteresting turnings and no particular merit.

BETTER

Right. Windsor armchair with mahogany arms, Rhode Island, eighteenth century. A good chair with fine turnings but with surprisingly crude arms. Note the brace back which consists of two spindles that rest on an extension of the back of the seat and serve to provide additional strength.

BETTER

Windsor armchair with mahogany arms, Rhode Island, eighteenth century. This chair would be fine if not for the thick plank shapeless seat.

BEST

Windsor armchair with mahogany arms, Rhode Island, eighteenth century. A superlative chair of the finest proportions and with every desirable feature. Note the fine shaping of the serpentine arms and the excellent saddle seat.

GOOD

Windsor armchair, Pennsylvania, eighteenth century. A country chair of mediocre quality.

BEST

Windsor armchair, Pennsylvania, eighteenth century. An outstanding chair—one of the best of its type. Most Windsors were originally painted and examples that retain the old black paint, as this one does, are especially prized. Note the magnificent turned legs which still retain the bulbous feet, a rare feature in itself. Also note the fine arm supports and the bold-shaped saddle seat.

GOOD

Left. Windsor bow-back side chair, New England, eighteenth century. A rustic chair of no particular merit or beauty.

BETTER

Right. Windsor bow-back side chair, New England, eighteenth century. An average chair of no great value.

BEST

Windsor bow-back side chair, New England, eighteenth century. An outstanding chair notable for its concave stretcher, an exceedingly rare and highly effective device.

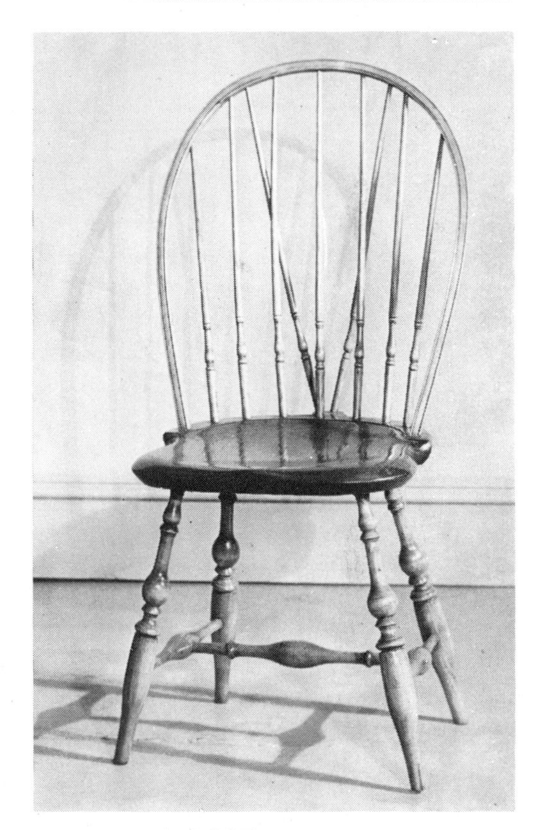

BEST

Windsor bow-back side chair, New England, eighteenth century. A perfect brace-back Rhode Island chair which will enhance the value of any collection. The bold ripe turnings and finely turned spindles show a master's touch.

GOOD

Windsor comb-back side chair with scrolled ears, New England, eighteenth century. A good chair but definitely suffers from comparison with the example shown below. The back does not have the fluency of the other chair, the stiles are not as well turned and do not have the same flare.

BEST

Windsor comb-back side chair with scrolled ears, New England, eighteenth century. A superlative chair with very finely turned stiles. Many collectors have comb-back chairs, but few indeed have examples of this quality.

GOOD

Windsor armchair with writing arm, New England, eighteenth century. Made by a carpenter, the antique value of this chair is nil.

BETTER

Windsor armchair with writing arm, New England, eighteenth century. A good chair but with turnings of lesser quality than those of the example shown below.

BEST

Windsor armchair with writing arm, New England, eighteenth century. An excellent chair with perfect turnings and a well-shaped saddle seat.

GOOD

Windsor comb-back writing armchair, New England, eighteenth century. Because of the great rarity of the chair shown below, some collectors would erroneously purchase an example such as this because it is also a writing-arm Windsor. Any price that was paid for this monstrosity would be too much, for it is not a work of art. It is ungainly, crudely executed and all its parts are thoroughly disjointed.

BEST

Windsor comb-back writing armchair, New England, eighteenth century. An outstanding chair of the quality which has given the writing-arm Windsor its deserved reputation as a collector's prize. It has every desirable feature including the handy drawer under the platform and seat.

GOOD

Windsor comb-back armchair, New England, eighteenth century. An average chair with indifferent turnings.

BEST

Windsor comb-back armchair with knuckle arms, New England, eighteenth century. A superlative chair which would excite the most discriminating collector. It has every desirable feature—the bold scroll ears, the fine knuckle arms, the well-shaped saddle seat and excellent turnings.

GOOD

Windsor comb-back armchair, Pennsylvania, eighteenth century. A spider-like chair of ungainly proportions. Note the lack of splay to the legs.

BEST

Windsor comb-back armchair, Pennsylvania, eighteenth century. A perfect chair with fine serpentine arm supports and the best Pennsylvania turnings.

GOOD

Windsor comb-back brace back armchair, New England, eighteenth century. Good chair but far from outstanding.

BEST

Windsor comb-back brace back armchair, New England, eighteenth century. A choice chair of excellent proportions. Note the finely scrolled ears, found on the best comb-back chairs.

GOOD

Windsor high chair, Pennsylvania, eighteenth century. A provincial attempt to emulate the great chair shown at bottom of page, but not crowned with success.

BETTER

Windsor high chair, Pennsylvania, eighteenth century. A very fine chair of beautiful proportions but without outstanding turnings.

BEST

Windsor high chair, Pennsylvania, eighteenth century. A masterpiece of Windsor chairmaking, this gem stands like a slender race horse. Its superb quality places it high in the ranks of the Windsor Who's Who. Note the bold rake to the superbly turned legs, the compact saddle seat and the balance between the back and the rest of the chair.

GOOD

Early turned daybed, Pennsylvania, circa 1680-1700. The turned legs and stretchers are far less interesting than those of the example shown below.

BEST

Early turned daybed, Pennsylvania, circa 1680-1700. An outstanding daybed with bold turnings of high quality, which afford an interesting contrast to the turnings of the above daybed.

BEST

Pilgrim turned daybed, New England, circa 1680-1700. The more slender New England type, this daybed displays the finest quality vase and ring turnings.

BEST

Early Queen Anne turned daybed with Spanish feet, New England, circa 1700-1720. The unusual double Queen Anne back and Spanish feet, together with the excellent turnings and proportion displayed throughout, place this daybed among the great rarities of its type.

BEST

Queen Anne walnut daybed, New England, circa 1720-1750. The violin-shaped splat, the yoke-shaped crest rail, the cabriole legs and turned stretchers all show a definite relationship to the conventional New England side chair of the period. A fine and rare example.

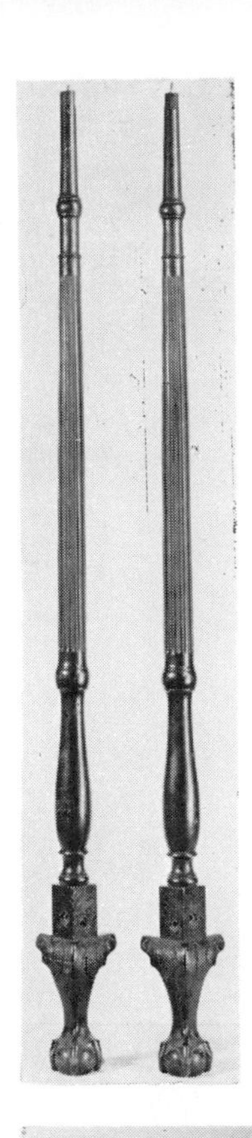

BETTER

Chippendale mahogany four-post bed, Philadelphia, circa 1750-1780. A good bed, but the bulbous section of the post is too long and not as finely shaped as the bed shown to the right.

BEST

Chippendale mahogany four-post bed, Newburyport, Mass., circa 1750-1780. The ultimate in an American bed, with beautifully formed posts and masterful deep carving. The carved kneecaps are removable. The original canvas attached to the head rail was stretched to the foot rail and laced to the sides. This bed was handed down in a Newburyport family and was once offered to Henry Ford for $50,000. It has since been purchased at a more sensible figure but the value is still high. It is now in a private collection.

BEST

Chippendale mahogany four-post bed, Philadelphia, circa 1750-1780. An outstanding example of a very rare type. The carved kneecaps are removable and the proportions of the foot posts are excellent.

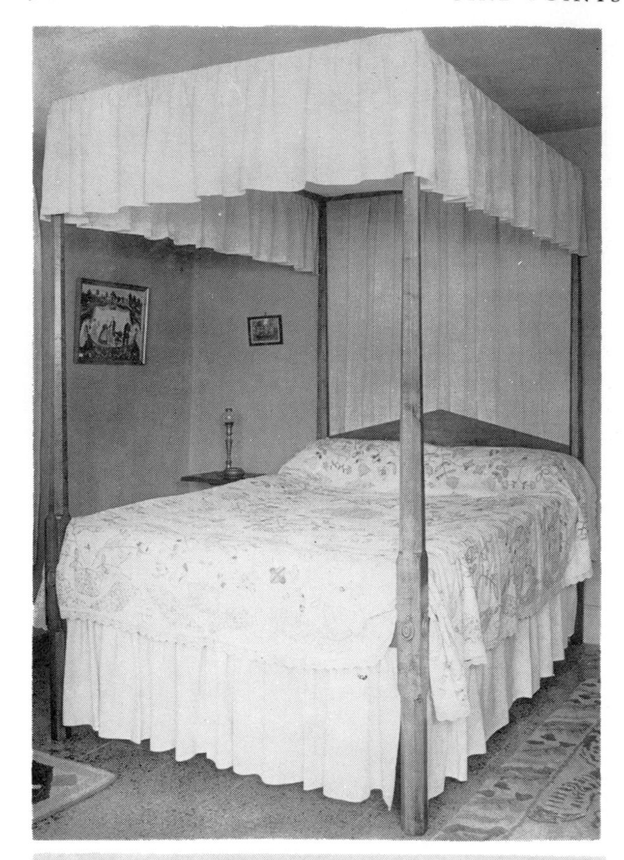

GOOD

Maple pencil-post bed, New England, circa 1750-1780. The relative desirability of these beds depends on the thinness of the posts. Those in this example are rather thick and heavy.

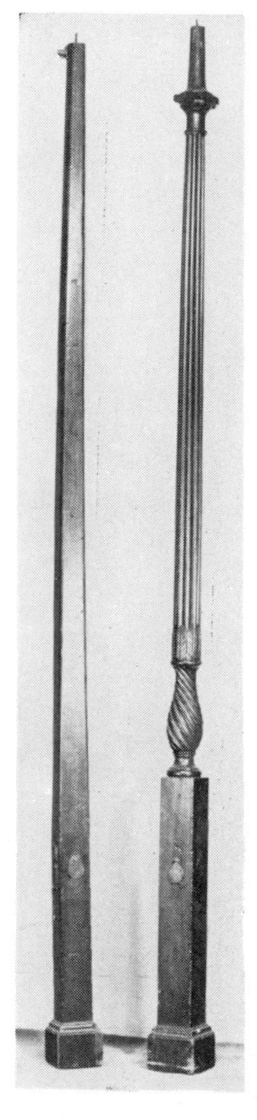

BEST

Chippendale mahogany four-post bed with Marlborough feet, attributed to John Goddard, Newport, R. I., circa 1750-1780. One of the outstanding beds of the period, complete with the original rails and head board (not shown in this picture). The spiral section effectively breaks the monotony of the reeded post, as does the horizontal platform above. This bed is now in a private collection.

BEST

Maple pencil-post bed, New England, circa 1750-1780. A highly desirable example with very slender posts that taper to hardly more than an inch in thickness at the top. This rare bed is in curly maple.

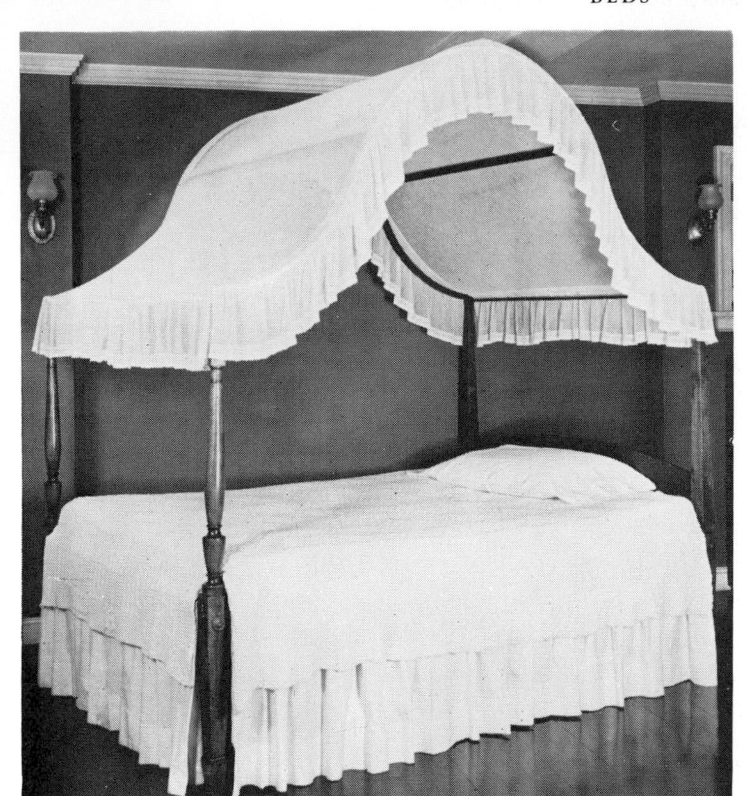

BEST

Hepplewhite field bed with spade feet and serpentine canopy, New England, circa 1780-1800. A beautiful bed with finely modeled foot posts. The unreeded foot post, not usually sought after by collectors, becomes highly prized when it is of this quality.

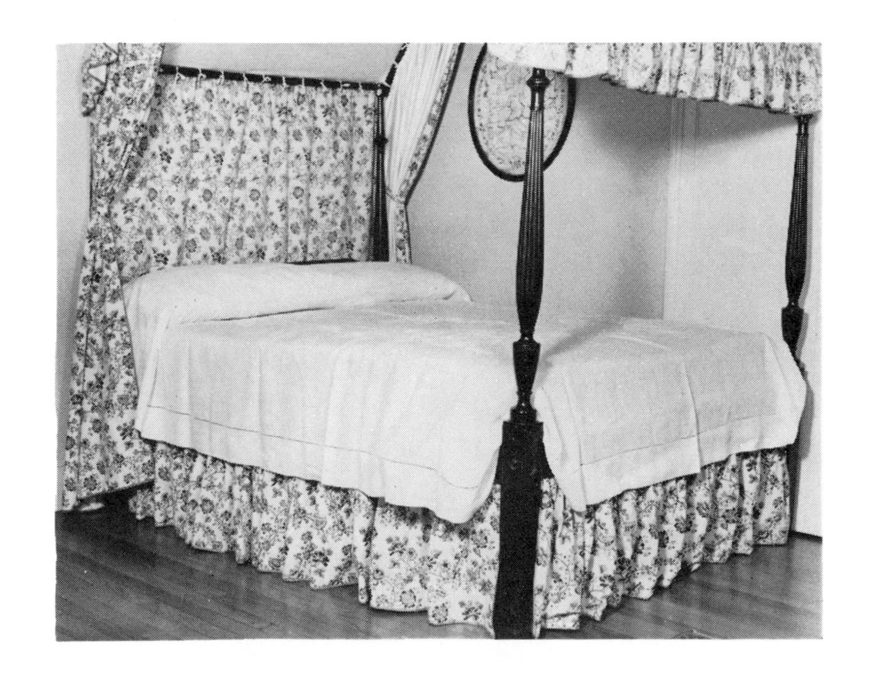

BEST

Hepplewhite mahogany inlaid field bed, New England, circa 1780-1800. An inlaid bed of this quality is of the utmost rarity. The urn is particularly well shaped.

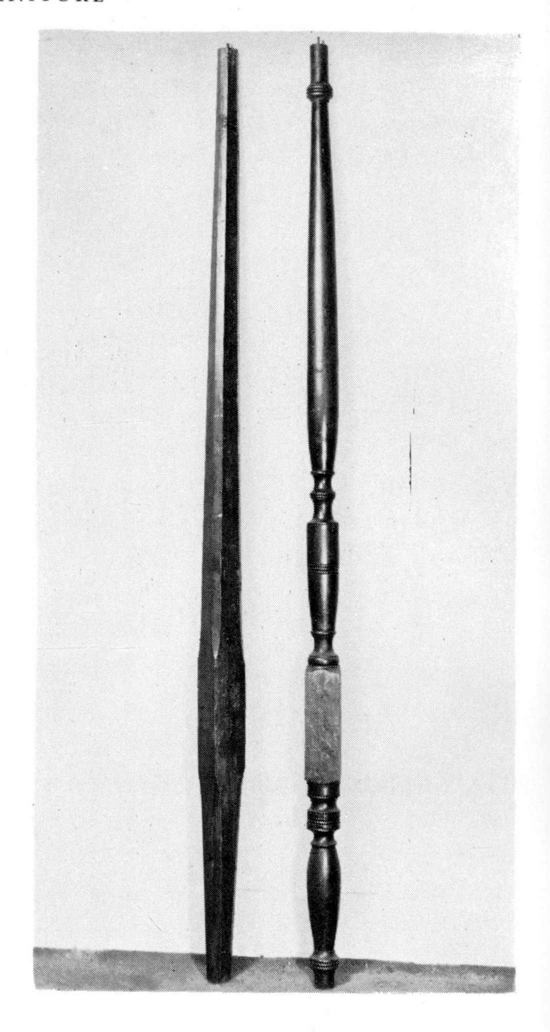

GOOD

Sheraton four-post bed, New England, circa 1800. A poorly designed post. The urn is too long and thick, the bulbous section is too thick at the top and the base has too many moldings.

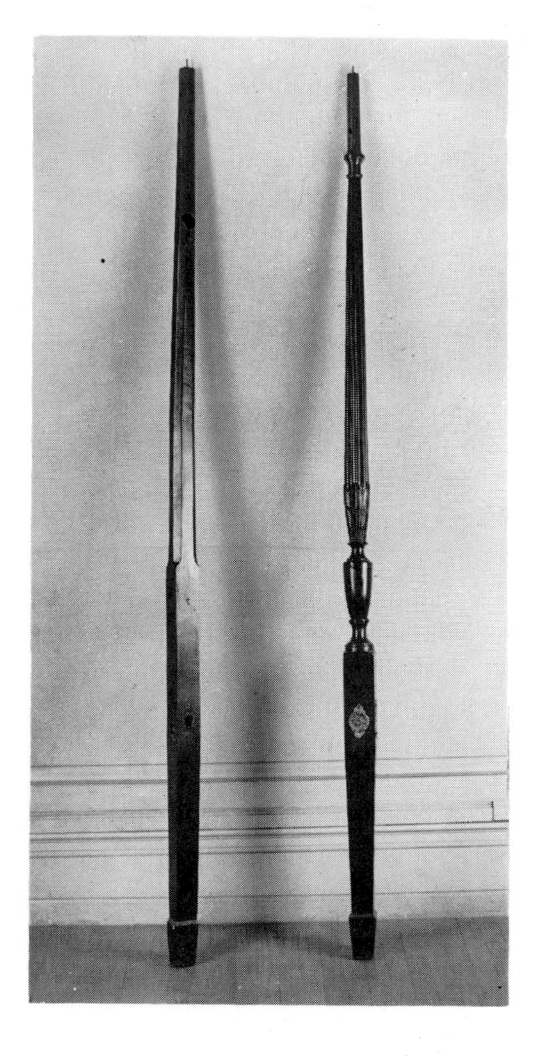

BEST

Sheraton four-post bed, New England, circa 1800. It is optional whether one calls this post Hepplewhite or Sheraton. That it is of superb proportion is the important factor. It provides an excellent contrast to the example shown above.

GOOD

Sheraton field bed, New England, circa 1800. A heavy, clumsy specimen.

BEST

Sheraton field bed, New England, circa 1800. A beautifully designed bed of excellent proportions which succeeds in every respect where the bed shown above fails—the bulbous turning of the legs, the shape of the urn, the bulbous post above the urn, the simpler but more gracefully designed headboard, the slender and delicate aspect of the bed as a whole. If the carving were stripped from this bed and transposed to the other, this bed would still be far superior. This illustrates the fact that detail becomes important only when it is combined with successful design.

GOOD

Sheraton field bed with bowed canopy, New England, circa 1800. An unsuccessful variation from the conventional. The designer would have done better to eliminate the turning above and below the reeding and to allow the reeding to flow into the rest of the post, as in the example shown below.

BEST

Sheraton field bed with bowed canopy, New England, circa 1800. This reeded bed is not only beautifully designed but is also important historically. Harriet Stark, whose name is inscribed on the head rail, was the wife of General Stark, the hero of the Battle of Bennington, Vermont, during the Revolutionary War. The bed is now in the Edison Institute, Dearborn, Michigan.

BETTER

Sheraton mahogany four-post bed, carved by Samuel McIntire, Salem, Mass., circa 1800. Fine carving, but a heavy reeded post compared with the bed shown below.

BEST

Sheraton mahogany four-post bed, carved by Samuel McIntire, Salem, Mass., circa 1800. A masterpiece—achieves the desired slenderness seldom found in beds of this type. The carving is of exceptional quality and depth. The frame canopy is the **original.**

BEST

Pilgrim bureau of oak and pine, New England, circa 1670-1700. The first of the four-drawer chests, this piece shows the care and ability exhibited in our earliest furniture. The geometric panels in each drawer give a pleasing effect.

BETTER

Chippendale straight-front bureau, with ogee bracket feet, New England, circa 1750-1780. A good conventional bureau, but too wide in relation to its height.

BEST

Chippendale straight-front bureau with ogee bracket feet, New England, circa 1750-1780. The exceptional quality and proportion of this bureau make it a valuable piece. Note how much more compact the body is compared with the example shown at left. The chamfered and fluted side and the finely molded top are unusual refinements.

BEST

Chippendale walnut bureau with fluted quarter columns, Philadelphia, circa 1750-1780. A fine quality bureau of a type produced in great number in and around Philadelphia. The proportions are good, the waist being not too wide, and the quarter columns help to make it appear more slender. The top is nicely molded and the ogee bracket feet are well shaped.

BEST

Chippendale mahogany serpentine-front bureau with stop-fluted columns, by Jonathan Gostelowe, Philadelphia, circa 1750-1780. A great masterpiece by an outstanding Philadelphia craftsman. The broad-shaped serpentine feet are indicative of this cabinetmaker. Note the superb mottled mahogany drawer fronts.

GOOD

Chippendale cherry oxbow bureau with ogee bracket feet, New England, circa 1750-1780. An average example with a weak curve. The wider body and the lack of overhang to the top make the proportions less successful than those of the compact example shown below.

BEST

Chippendale mahogany oxbow bureau with ogee bracket feet, New England, circa 1750-1780. A very choice example of perfect proportions. Note how the serpentine curve stops before the edge of the drawer and follows into the bracket of the foot, creating a bolder and more compressed curve.

BETTER

Chippendale walnut serpentine-front bureau with claw and ball feet, New England, circa 1750-1780. An average example of good but not outstanding quality. The single-serpentine-curved front does not generally command the price of the double-serpentine-front type shown below, since it is not as forceful a design. The claw and ball feet are not as well formed as those of the other example.

BEST

Chippendale walnut serpentine-front bureau with claw and ball feet, New England, circa 1750-1780. An outstanding bureau of fine proportions. The center ornament is most effective and the claw and ball feet are the finest quality.

Close-up of claw and ball foot. Note the strength with which the slender ankle holds the claw, the fullness of the ball and the sharp grasp of the knuckles.

BEST

Chippendale mahogany serpentine-front bureau, with claw and ball feet, New England, circa 1750-1780. A compact bureau of small size which cannot fail to satisfy the most discriminating collector. The usual criticism of the single-serpentine-front is not present here. In order to create a bolder serpentine, the curve is compressed into a smaller section, and the bracket of the foot follows the beginning of the curve, thereby accentuating it. The side brasses were used only on the more expensive bureaus of the period.

BEST

Chippendale mahogany bombé-front bureau with claw and ball feet, New England, circa 1750-1780. An American classic. The bombé shape is of Dutch origin, but only in America were the examples carved from solid mahogany as this is. The sides are hewn from one solid log as are the blocked serpentine drawer fronts. It is interesting to note that if the sides of this bureau were straight, the shape of the front would be identical with that of the bureau shown at top left.

BEST

Chippendale mahogany bombé-front bureau with ogee bracket feet, New England, circa 1750-1780. Now in the Edison Institute. The fine proportion and quality of this great piece are apparent. Note the superb selection of solid figured mahogany used on the drawer fronts. The rococco chased brasses are exceptionally florid for an American piece.

BETTER

Chippendale mahogany block-front bureau, New England, circa 1750-1780. The round block of this somewhat abused example is perceptibly weaker than those of the two other examples on this page.

BEST

Chippendale mahogany block-front bureau, New England, circa 1750-1780. A well-proportioned example with a bold round block. Note how the inner portion of the foot follows the contour of the block.

BEST

Chippendale mahogany block-front bureau, New England, circa 1750-1780. An exceptional example with fine mottled mahogany fronts and large bold original brasses.

BEST

Chippendale mahogany block-front bureau, Newport, R. I., circa 1750-1780. An American classic and one of the best block-front bureaus from every standpoint. It is now in a private collection.

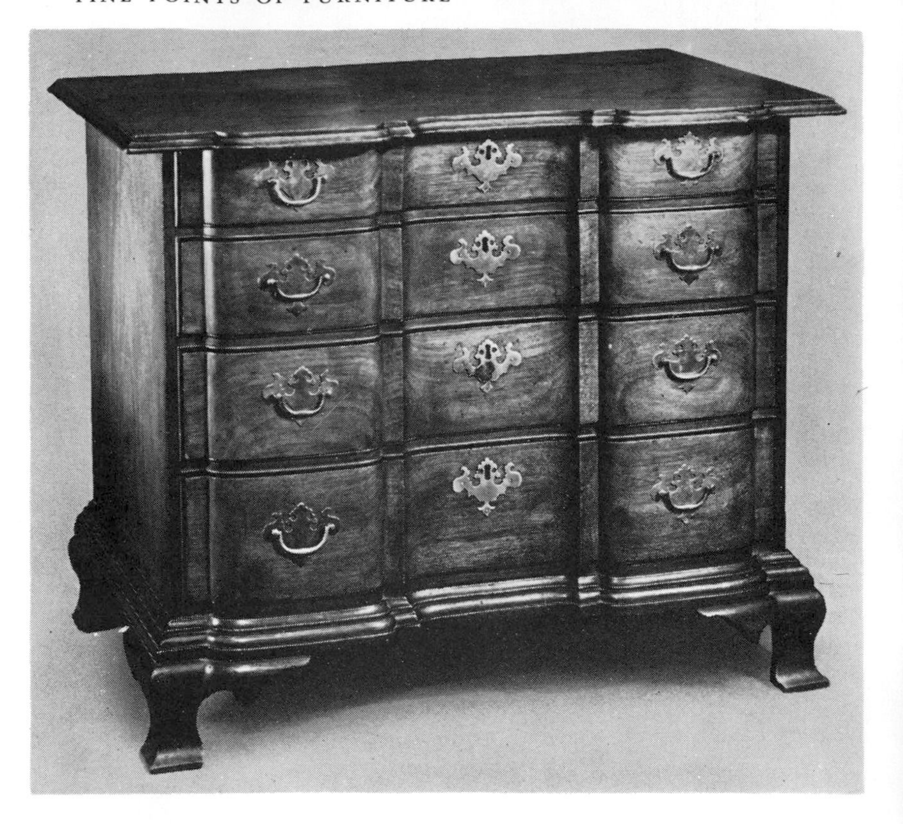

Side view of bureau. A cabinetmaker can fully appreciate the quality of these dovetails, but it requires no specialized knowledge to appreciate the boldness of the blocking and the superlative molding at the top and base. Note the single plank of solid figured mahogany used for the side.

BEST

Chippendale mahogany block-front bureau, New England, circa 1750-1780. The best New England cabinetmakers combined a deep love of simplicity with exquisite craftsmanship in the finest mahogany. The fact is that hundreds of these bureaus were made throughout New England prior to the Revolution and were so compact, useful and beautiful and so durably constructed that a large number have survived intact. In spite of this, they are highly prized and command a substantial figure whenever one appears on the market.

BEST

Chippendale mahogany block and shell bureau, by Goddard or Townsend, Newport, R. I., circa 1750-1780. A priceless example of the Newport school. The C scroll on the leg is a feature used in conjunction with the shell-carved furniture of Goddard and the Townsends. A study of this fully developed shell will indicate why it is considered the most important motif of distinctly American design.

GOOD

Hepplewhite cherry straight-front bureau, New England, circa 1780-1800. A mediocre example with an ambitious but crudely shaped apron. A straight-front bureau of the Hepplewhite period cannot fail to appear more boxy than the bow-front variety. If the quality and detail of this bureau were as fine as in the bureau below, it would still have less value.

BEST

Hepplewhite mahogany bow-front bureau, New England, circa 1780-1800. A choice bureau with a finely shaped apron. Note the more subtle lines in this bow-front bureau than in the straight-front example above. The cross-banded borders relieve the broad expanse of the drawer fronts.

GOOD

Hepplewhite cherry straight-front bureau, New England, circa 1780-1800. A country bureau with little to distinguish it. Note the crude apron which, however, is slightly more refined than that of the one at top right.

GOOD

Hepplewhite straight-front bureau, New England, circa 1780-1800. A hopelessly crude apron on an inferior bureau.

BETTER

Hepplewhite mahogany bow-front bureau, New England, circa 1780-1800. This more sophisticated example still suffers from an ineptly shaped apron.

BEST

Hepplewhite mahogany bow-front bureau, New England, circa 1780-1800. A bureau of the finest quality and proportions, worth many times more than any of the other examples shown on this page. Note the refined contour of the apron and the flare of the outer edge of the foot. The top has a thin line of inlay at the upper and lower edges and a checkered line in the center to relieve the thick appearance apparent in the other bureaus. The beaded edges of the drawers are present in the better bureaus of this period.

GOOD

Hepplewhite curly maple bow-front bureau, New England, circa 1780-1800. The fact that curly maple bow-front bureaus are rare does not make this poorly proportioned piece valuable. On puny feet with a thick heavy top, it would not be considered at any price by a discriminating collector.

BEST

Hepplewhite curly maple bow-front bureau, New England, circa 1780-1800. An outstanding example of a very rare type. Surprisingly few curly maple bow-front bureaus have been found. The scrolling of the apron is delightful, as are the proportions and quality of workmanship.

GOOD

Hepplewhite mahogany and satinwood bureau, Salem, Mass., circa 1780-1800. A feeble application of satinwood panels at the drawer ends which were better eliminated, for it adds nothing to the beauty of the bureau.

BEST

Hepplewhite mahogany and satinwood bureau, Salem, Mass., circa 1780-1800. Another masterpiece. It is understandable how the great satinwood school of Salem developed, as it was an important shipping port and the select mahogany and satinwood were brought in from the Indies. Note how carefully the flame figure is matched in the center panels. The cross-banding bordering each panel is effective and difficult to construct. The matching shaving mirror is a great rarity.

BEST

Hepplewhite mahogany and satinwood bureau, Salem, Mass., circa 1780-1800. An American classic—the ultimate in a satinwood-front bureau. The oval center panels are a rare and beautiful feature. Note how each is framed by triangular veneered panels.

The following group (pages 108-111) is comprised of a series of oak and pine Pilgrim chests all fashioned within the first hundred years of our colonization. Certainly the early settlers retained the general form of the carved Elizabethan chests with which they were familiar in the Mother Country, but their original interpretations of the carved fronts and split spindles show the early emergence of the distinctive American character. The large number of fine specimens which have survived prove that there were many more families of wealth and culture than is generally believed. The American quartered oak, from which these chests were fashioned, is definitely lighter in color and tone than its English counterpart. Those few chests which have not been scraped and refinished over the many generations present an invaluable opportunity to see the handiwork of the Pilgrims in its most desirable aspect. They represent the roots of the American character in the first cultural stage of its development. For this reason are they so highly prized.

BEST

Carved chest, by Nicholas Disbrowe, Hartford, Conn., circa 1650-1680. The earliest signed piece of American craftsmanship. Inscription on back of lower drawer reads: "Mary Allyn's chistt cutte and joyned by Nich: Disbrowe." Nicholas Disbrowe was born in England in 1612; he was the son of a joiner. It is indeed fortunate that this invaluable record of Pilgrim craftsmanship should be discovered on such a superb chest fashioned by one of the finest carvers and joiners of the Pilgrim era. Disbrowe is considered the stylistic parent of the Hadley chests, which probably were made by apprentices in his shop who moved to Hadley and Northampton, Massachusetts, a generation later.

BEST

Tulip and sunflower chest, Connecticut, circa 1670-1700. One of the greatest of all American chests, it is purely American in design and character. The carving is fine and deep, with a punchwork background. The bold and finely formed split spindles are ebonized to provide contrast. Now in the Edison Institute.

BEST

Hadley chest, vicinity of Hadley, Mass., circa 1670-1700. A two-drawer example with the initials H.M. The little scroll terminals on the initials and throughout the carving are typical of this kind of chest. Examples of Pilgrim furniture must retain their old aspect to be desired by collectors. Pieces which have been refinished or scraped lose much of their value.

BEST

Dower chest, New England, circa 1670-1700. A great masterpiece of American design. The original red paint and floral sprays in the panels have been preserved for over two hundred and fifty years.

BEST

Chest with split spindles, Connecticut, circa 1670-1700. A simpler chest than the one below, it shows the bold and vigorous character of its creator. The turnings of the split spindles are exceptionally fine.

BEST

Chest with geometric panels, Massachusetts, circa 1670-1700. Another masterpiece of Pilgrim furniture. The triangular notching is exceptional, as is the beauty of the three geometric panels.

BEST

Pilgrim oak court cupboard with geometric panels and split spindles, New England, circa 1670-1700. One of the most important types of Pilgrim furniture, this well-preserved example is a priceless rarity. The few such cupboards that were made stood in the finest homes of the period.

BEST

Pilgrim oak tulip and sunflower-carved court cupboard, Connecticut, circa 1670-1700. Probably the greatest American court cupboard, this example now in the Boston Museum of Fine Arts shows the development of a distinctive American character in our earliest furniture. The superb carving and inspired design are remarkable. Courtesy of Museum of Fine Arts, Boston, M. & M. Karolik Collection.

BETTER

Pilgrim painted court cupboard, New England, circa 1670-1700. The crudity of this cupboard, as pointed up by the beauty of the example shown below, is evident.

BEST

Pilgrim painted court cupboard, New England, circa 1670-1700. Now in the Edison Institute. A unique and exceptional cupboard which bears the full name of its original owner—Hannah Barnard. The beauty and intricacy of the painted design is worthy of study.

BEST

Early open cupboard with scalloped sides and top, Pennsylvania, circa 1700-1720. One of the best examples of this rare type. Such cupboards or dressers are sought by collectors only when the scalloping is original and has not been reshaped at a later date, as has often been done. A rescalloped piece is no better than a reproduction.

BEST

Left. Corner cupboard with shell dome and stop-fluted pilasters, Rhode Island, circa 1750-1780. One of the outstanding shell cupboards. The arched panel in the door is very effective.

BEST

Right. Corner cupboard with shell dome and fluted pilasters, American, circa 1750-1780. Open view of a very fine cupboard.

CHESTS-ON-CHESTS

BEST

Chippendale maple chest-on-chest with claw and ball feet, New England, circa 1750-1780. A very fine piece of desirable small size. Few maple chests-on-chests are of this quality. The finely modeled claw and ball feet, the excellence of the moldings and the slender proportions indicate the hand of a fine craftsman.

BEST

Chippendale cherry chest-on-chest with broken arch top, Connecticut, circa 1750-1780. This vigorous top with the bold shell and finely carved rosettes is among the best of the Connecticut variety.

BEST

Chippendale cherry chest-on-chest with fretwork scroll top, Connecticut, circa 1750-1780. This attractive piece is unusually small for its type, which makes it more adaptable to the limited space requirements of the homes of today. It is beautifully proportioned, with an exceptionally fine fretwork design. The upper portion of this fretwork indicates the handiwork of Eliphalet Chapin.

BEST

Chippendale cherry chest-on-chest with broken arch top, Connecticut, circa 1750-1780. The crowning achievement of the Connecticut chest-on-chest. The proportions and quality leave nothing to be desired. The spiral rope columns, the three magnificent carved fans in the upper drawers and the unusual motif under the center finial all add to the beauty and therefore the importance of this great piece.

BEST

Chippendale bonnet-top chest-on-chest, New England, circa 1750-1780. A piece so perfect in proportion and quality that it would outrank an average example of a more important type. The shape of the bonnet is one of the most satisfying, having just the right curve to the molding and just the right opening between. The carved fan is bold and deep and the fluted pilasters are always effective. An outstanding and rare piece.

BEST

Chippendale mahogany block-front chest-on-chest with bonnet top, New England, circa 1750-1780. This great masterpiece is one of a very few examples made with the recessed cupboard in the lower section. It is perfection in design and detail. The gilding of the fans, pilasters and finials is most unusual.

BEST

Chippendale mahogany serpentine-front chest-on-chest with broken arch top, attributed to Benjamin Frothingham, Charlestown, Mass., circa 1750-1780. Now in the Edison Institute. An American classic and one of the best of the American chests-on-chests. The proportions are unusually successful. The carved rosettes are unique and the blocked ogee bracket feet are most unusual and effective. The distinctive blocking of the top drawer of the lower section is present in a labeled desk by Frothingham.

GOOD

Chippendale block-front cherry chest-on-chest with bonnet top, New England, circa 1750-1780. The fact that a piece of this type in cherry is very rare does not keep this chest from being mediocre and of less value than the straight-front chest illustrated on the right-hand side of page 115. The top is not narrower than the base as in the finer New England chests-on-chests, which makes it appear heavy and cumbersome. The bonnet is cramped and poorly designed.

BETTER

Chippendale mahogany block-front chest-on-chest with bonnet top, New England, circa 1750-1780. The quality of this piece is excellent and the blocking is bold and fine. The top has one long drawer more than is usually found, which makes the top appear too tall in relation to the base. Also the fluted columns have no platforms below or moldings above as in the example at bottom left. The brasses are exceptional.

BEST

Chippendale mahogany block-front chest-on-chest with broken arch top. Made in 1774 for Mary Hidden of Marblehead, Mass., for her wedding linen and purchased from one of her descendants. An American classic. The perfection of form, proportion and detail make it one of the great American chests-on-chests. Note the superbly modeled claw and ball feet, the slide in the lower section, the slope of the two end top drawers which follows the contour of the arch and the finely carved rosettes.

BEST

Chippendale mahogany chest-on-chest with broken arch top, Philadelphia, circa 1750-1780. One of the finest and most important Philadelphia chests-on-chests. The bold carved shell and vines are done by a master carver as are the excellent finials and center cartouche. This piece has exceptional proportions, not having too wide a body. The fluted quarter columns further lighten the appearance. The broken arch top has a beautiful curve.

BEST

Chippendale mahogany chest-on-chest with broken arch top, Philadelphia, circa 1750-1780. One of the great Philadelphia chests-on-chests with a magnificent carved top.

GOOD

Grandfather clock with broken arch top, Pennsylvania, circa 1760-1780. A crude example with a weak curve to the arch and an unskillful raised panel in the base. A clock of little value.

BETTER

Grandfather clock with broken arch top, Pennsylvania, dated 1799. While this clock is not the most sophisticated in workmanship or proportion, it has a great deal of charm and appeal. The carving of the date in the raised panel is possibly unique.

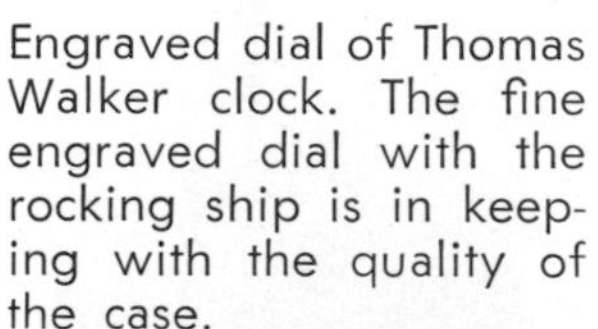

Engraved dial of Thomas Walker clock. The fine engraved dial with the rocking ship is in keeping with the quality of the case.

BEST

Chippendale mahogany grandfather clock with broken arch top, dial signed Thomas Walker, Fredericksburg, Va., circa 1750-1780. The case was probably made to order in Philadelphia. One of the outstanding American clocks, it has a unique hooded top which is an architectural gem. The length of the waist aids the proportion of the clock, even though it eliminates its potential use in the average present-day home. Courtesy of Museum of Fine Arts, Boston, M. & M. Karolik Collection.

BETTER

Chippendale grandfather clock with carved hood, Lancaster County, Pa., by Martin Schreiner, Lancaster, Pa., circa 1760-1780. An excellent comparison of two clocks from the standpoint of proportion. The association of the craftsmanship of the two clocks is evident. Apparently Martin Schreiner had an order for a shorter clock than the one made by the Farrars, but he sacrificed proportion to accomplish this—to the detriment of the clock. If he had designed a smaller base and hood to conform to the abbreviated waist, he would have created an outstanding clock.

BEST

Chippendale grandfather clock with carved hood, Lancaster County, Pa., by C. & D. Farrar, Lampeter, Pa., circa 1760-1780. A very fine clock with typical Lancaster carving. The slender waist of ample length keeps the hood from appearing top-heavy, as happens in clock at left. The proportions are excellent.

GOOD

Chippendale mahogany grandfather clock with broken arch top, vicinity of Philadelphia, circa 1750-1780. A less sophisticated case with a poorly designed hood.

BETTER

Chippendale mahogany grandfather clock with broken arch top, Philadelphia, circa 1750-1780. The arch of this clock is too high and stiff. Otherwise it is an excellent example of the Philadelphia school, with good proportions, a slender waist and a fine raised panel in the base.

BEST

Left. Chippendale mahogany grandfather clock with broken arch top, by Huston, Philadelphia, circa 1760-1780. A masterpiece of stately proportions and excellent quality. The shaped raised panel in the base is of fine workmanship, the carving in the hood and the curve of the broken arch top are in the best Philadelphia tradition.

BEST

Right. Chippendale mahogany grandfather clock with broken arch top, Philadelphia, circa 1760-1780. A most important example of the Philadelphia school. The hood is well executed with a fine broken arch top and fretwork carving. The carved rooster finial is not primitive but is rather the proud achievement of a master carver.

GOOD

Left. Chippendale cherry block and shell grandfather clock, Newport, R. I., circa 1750-1780, works by Squire Millard, Warwick, R. I. The least refined case of the three Newport clocks on this page and consequently the least valuable in spite of the finely engraved dial. The carved shell is attractive but not as fully developed as in the two other examples and not as representative of Goddard or Townsend handiwork. The door and the square panel in the base should each cover a larger surface. Note the crudity of the fluted pilasters in the hood.

BETTER

Left. Chippendale mahogany block and shell grandfather clock, case by J. Goddard or Townsend, Newport, R. I., circa 1750-1780. A fine clock with the typical and important carved shell of the Newport school. The body appears somewhat wide, and a great deal of the effectiveness of the blocked section is lost by the large plain area surrounding it.

BEST

Chippendale mahogany block and shell grandfather clock, by John Goddard or Townsend, Newport, R. I., circa 1760-1780. The ultimate in a clock of the Goddard school. The appearance of heaviness present in the clock at bottom left is relieved not only by the length of the waist but also by the fluted quarter columns and the chamfered corners of the base. The broken arch hood with the typical Goddard rosettes and finials adds to the beauty and importance of this priceless clock.

GOOD

Cherry grandfather clock with broken arch top, American, circa 1780-1800. A country clock of mediocre quality. The waist is too wide and there is nothing to relieve the monotony of the large plain surfaces. Many collectors attempt to excuse the purchase of cheap clocks such as this by saying they love simplicity. Simplicity is never a virtue unless combined with dignity.

BEST

Cherry inlaid grandfather clock with broken arch top, by George Woltz, Hagerstown, Md., circa 1780-1800. An outstanding clock which was made for the prominent Ridgeley family of Maryland and stood in the Ridgeley house. It is of slender, graceful proportion with well-placed inlay of fine quality. The scrolled fretwork top with the dentil moldings is a masterpiece of design and execution. In a private collection.

BEST

Mahogany grandfather clock with blocked door, made by Simon Willard as an apprentice in Benjamin Willard's shop, Roxbury, Mass., 1772. This beautiful clock was long considered to be the work of Benjamin Willard, Simon's older brother, since his name is inscribed on the dial. Not until this clock was sold to a private collector and the brass works taken apart for cleaning was the inscription (shown at bottom of page 125) found written in Simon's handwriting. It followed that Simon made the works in his brother Benjamin's shop, and since he had not yet earned the title of master clockmaker was not able to sign his name on the dial. Sixty-four years passed and Simon had become the most famous clockmaker in New England, the inventor of the banjo clock and the lighthouse clock. His many pupils had emulated his style, resulting in the great school of New England clockmaking. He was now a venerable old man still hard at work when in 1833 the clock came into his shop for cleaning. With emotion he recognized it as one of his first efforts whose excellence he could well be proud of. With trembling hand he inscribed on the works: "Made by Simon Willard in his seventeenth year. Cleaned by him in August 10, 1833, in his eighty-first year."

With this great discovery the mystery of the stamped pendulum bob was solved. Stamped in the lead were the names of Simon Willard and John Morris. It had been known that Simon Willard had been apprenticed to an Englishman named Morris when he was thirteen years old, but no trace could be found of this Morris. Since three or four identical stamped pendulum bobs have been found on early Willard clocks, it is logical to assume that Simon Willard and his teacher, John Morris, planned to go into partnership and prepared a stamp which they would impress on all their clocks. Apparently the partnership never materialized. Meanwhile, although Simon's brother Benjamin already had a shop, he was new in the clockmaking business. Sometime between 1764 and 1770 he moved to Grafton, Massachusetts, and set up shop and in December, 1771, he moved to Roxbury, where this clock was made. The influence of the Hartford school of clockmakers on Benjamin and Simon in this embryo stage of their careers now becomes clearer, for this clock case is identical in design with two or three known Connecticut clocks of the period. A mantel clock marked Simon Willard, Grafton, shows unmistakable Connecticut design. The brass engraved dial and the moon phase with the blue background show a definite association with the typical Connecticut clock of the same period. Also, it has just been discovered that Simon Willard's teacher, John Morris, lived in Hartford, Connecticut.

This remarkable clock is an important link connecting two noteworthy schools of American clockmaking, the Connecticut school dominated by Thomas Harland and the Boston school dominated by Simon Willard. This definite association has never before been fully established.

Stamped pendulum bob dated 1770 and 1771, undoubtedly the years of Simon Willard's and Morris' proposed partnership.

Brass engraved dial, inscribed: "Benjamin Willard, Roxbury, Warranted for Mr. James Mears, 1772." During this period the dials were made locally, and this one was probably engraved by a prominent silversmith of Boston. Later on it became the practice to import the enamel dials from England, but the brass works during all periods were made in this country. Note the engraved eagles under the name. They indicate the growing spirit of defiance of the Mother Country brewing at the time.

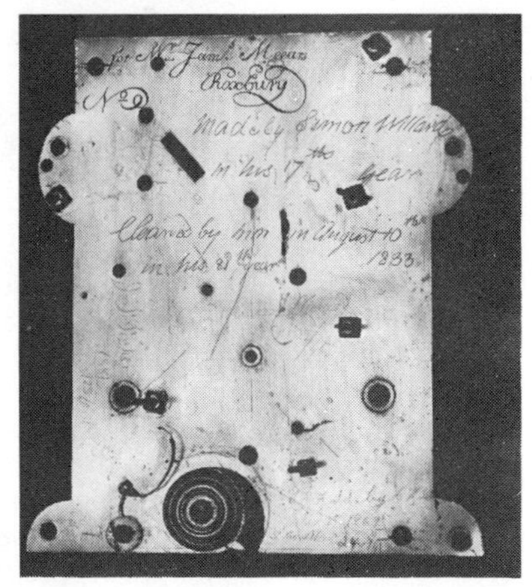

Simon Willard's inscription on clock works.

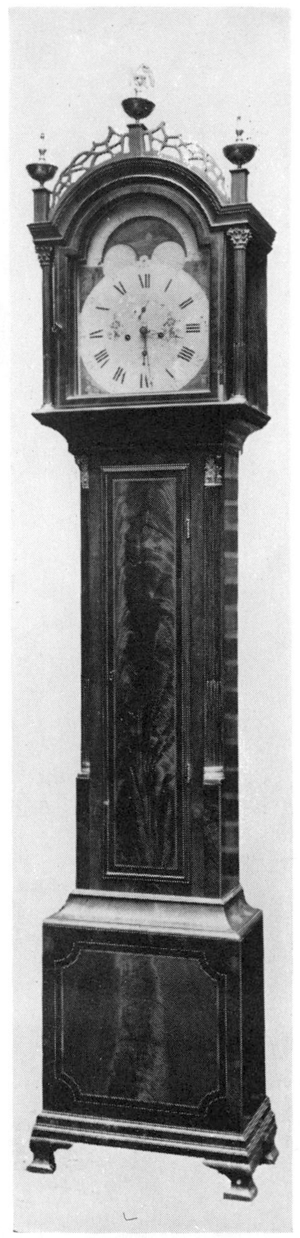

BEST

Mahogany grandfather clock with fretwork top, by Simon Willard, Roxbury, Mass., circa 1790-1800. A beautiful example and one of Simon's more ambitious productions. Simon Willard did not make his own cases but contracted for the work as did practically all the contemporary clock-makers. Certain cabinetmakers specialized in making cases for the various makers, which accounts for the similarity in design of the clocks of different artisans. The stately proportions are exemplary—the draped panel in the base and the brass Corinthian capitals of the columns are outstanding.

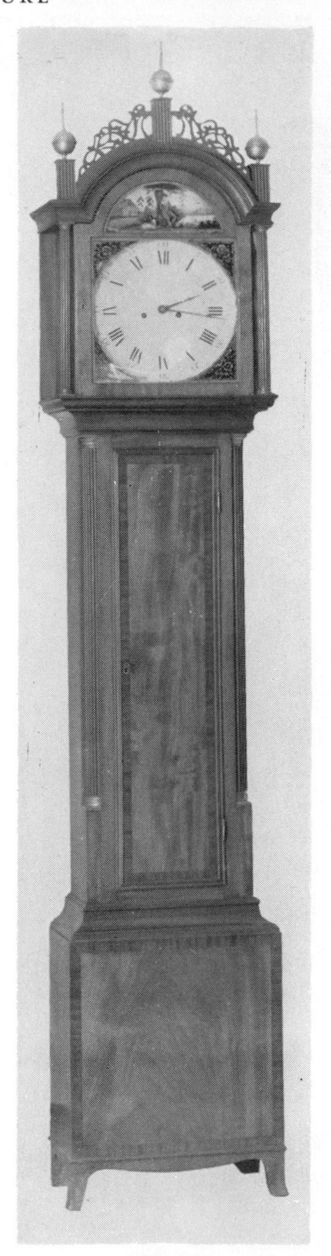

BEST

Mahogany grandfather clock, by Aaron Willard, Roxbury, Mass., circa 1790-1800. A great masterpiece by Simon's brother. The upper portion of the glass door has a painted landscape, to our knowledge a unique and attractive feature. The proportions and quality leave nothing to be desired.

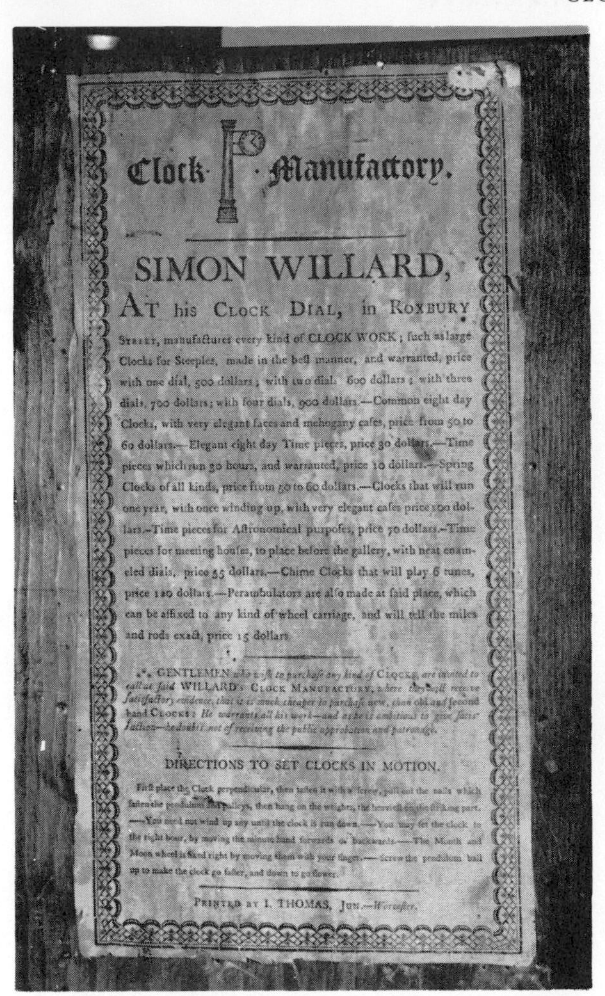

Clock Manufactory.

SIMON WILLARD,

AT his CLOCK DIAL, in ROXBURY

STREET, manufactures every kind of CLOCK WORK; ſuch as large Clocks for Steeples, made in the beſt manner, and warranted, price with one dial, 500 dollars; with two dials 600 dollars; with three dials, 700 dollars; with four dials, 900 dollars.—Common eight day Clocks, with very elegant faces and mahogany caſes, price from 50 to 60 dollars.—Elegant eight day Time pieces, price 30 dollars.—Time pieces which run 30 hours, and warranted, price 10 dollars.—Spring Clocks of all kinds, price from 50 to 60 dollars.—Clocks that will run one year, with once winding up, with very elegant caſes price 100 dollars.—Time pieces for Aſtronomical purpoſes, price 70 dollars.—Time pieces for meeting houſes, to place before the gallery, with neat enameled dials, price 55 dollars.—Chime Clocks that will play 6 tunes, price 120 dollars.—Perambulators are alſo made at ſaid place, which can be affixed to any kind of wheel carriage, and will tell the miles and rods exact, price 15 dollars.

*** GENTLEMEN *who wiſh to purchaſe any kind of* CLOCKS, *are invited to call at ſaid* WILLARD's CLOCK MANUFACTORY, *where they will receive ſatisfactory evidence, that it is much cheaper to purchaſe new, than old and ſecond* hand CLOCKS: *He warrants all his work—and as he is ambitious to give ſatisfaction—he doubts not of receiving the public approbation and patronage.*

DIRECTIONS TO SET CLOCKS IN MOTION.

First place the Clock perpendicular, then faſten it with a ſcrew, pull out the nails which faſten the pendulum [illegible] pulleys, then hang on the weights, the heavieſt on the ſtriking part.—You need not wind up any until the clock is run down.—You may ſet the clock to the right hour, by moving the minute hand forwards or backwards.—The Month and Moon wheel is fixed right by moving them with your finger.—Screw the pendulum ball up to make the clock go faſter, and down to go ſlower.

PRINTED BY I. THOMAS, JUN.—*Worceſter.*

Label on inside of door of Simon Willard clock. This label appears on many Simon Willard clocks; those which command a high price are expected to have the label. It gives directions for setting up the clock and the prices of the various types. Willard's typical grandfather clock originally cost from fifty to sixty dollars.

BEST

Mahogany grandfather clock with fan inlay and fretwork top, by Simon Willard, Roxbury, Mass., circa 1780-1800. One of Simon Willard's best clocks, of compact size and dynamic proportions. This clock has Simon Willard's signature on the back of the moon dial. It is now in a private collection and still keeping perfect time. The fan inlay in the corners is an effective and rare touch, the fretwork is a beautiful design and the fluted brass finials conform with the fluted supporting plinths. This is a presentation clock and is inscribed on the dial: "Warranted for Mr. Thomas Thompson"—the original owner.

GOOD

Grandfather clock, Boston or vicinity, circa 1790-1800. A crude example which shows the obvious influence of the great Willard school but not the same ability or effort as a typical Willard example. Note the particularly crude base and feet and the heavy, ineptly done fretwork. The fluted quarter columns and hood columns do not contain the brass stop flutes and the columns begin at the base of the door instead of part way up, as in the other two clocks shown on this page.

BETTER

Mahogany grandfather clock, by Aaron Willard, Roxbury, Mass., circa 1790-1800. A fine clock except for a surprisingly weak base which does not conform in quality with the rest of the clock.

BEST

Mahogany inlaid grandfather clock, by Ephraim Willard, Boston, Mass., circa 1800. An outstanding clock by Simon Willard's gifted brother, who made very few clocks. This is perhaps the best example made by him. It has the desirable rocking ship dial and the original bill of sale. The quality is unsurpassed. The inlaid ovals in the door and base add interest to the design, as does the cross-banded border of the door. The base with its finer molding and well-formed ogee bracket is much more beautiful than that of the center clock.

GOOD

Half high clock, by unknown maker, New England, circa 1820. The fact that this type clock is extremely rare does not make valuable this hopelessly crude example. It lives on the reputation of its finer contemporaries.

BEST

Half high clock, by W. Shearman, Andover, Mass., circa 1800-1810. One of few examples of this rare type which has the delicate fretwork more frequently found on the contemporary grandfather's clocks. It is beautifully proportioned with a narrow waist and fine cross-banded borders. This clock stands forty-nine inches high. It is a priceless specimen.

BEST

Half high clock, by Joshua Wilder, Hingham, Mass., circa 1800-1810. An exceptional and coveted example by the best-known maker of this type. It is more sophisticated than some examples by this maker, but any original specimen is highly desirable. The proportions are admirable and the scrolled apron and nicely flaring French feet form a most desirable base. The particularly fine figured mahogany, the raised molded edge of the door, and the flanking quarter columns are rare refinements.

BEST

Mahogany shelf clock, with brass dial engraved by Simon Willard, Roxbury, Mass., circa 1770-1775. A great rarity by the Dean of American clock-makers. The relation to the earliest Simon Willard grandfather clock, illustrated on page 125, is apparent, as each has the same unusual blocked feet. This clock was made within the first few years of Simon's business career and shows the quality he demanded from the very beginning. Simon made very few shelf clocks.

BEST

Mahogany inlaid shelf clock with kidney-shaped dial, by James Dakin, Boston or vicinity, circa 1780-1790. A beautifully proportioned example which combines simplicity with dignity. The shape of the section under the circular dial is identical with that of the early Simon Willard shelf clock, illustrated at left, showing the source of Mr. Dakin's inspiration.

BETTER

Inlaid shelf clock with fluted columns and arched door, broken arch top and brass dial, by B. C. Gilman, Exeter, N. H., circa 1790. The similarity of design to that of the clock at right is immediately apparent. However, the elongated case detracts from the compact proportions evident in the David Wood clock. Also the broken arch top is cruder. This is a desirable clock but not as fine or nearly as valuable as the other.

BEST

Inlaid shelf clock with fluted columns and arched door, broken arch top and brass dial, by David Wood, Newburyport, Mass., circa 1790. An American classic of superlative proportions by the greatest exponent of the shelf clock. It forms an interesting comparison with the clock at left, for it illustrates the folly of judging desirability solely by type. The superior treatment of the identical medium makes this clock worth several times the price of the Gilman clock.

BETTER

Cherry inlaid shelf clock with kidney-shaped dial, by Boynton, Boston or vicinity, circa 1790-1800. A clock of medium quality. The provincial workmanship is immediately apparent upon comparison with the David Wood clock illustrated at right. They each have rectangular doors in the base, but the door to this clock lacks the finely molded border and the cross-banding, as well as the quarter round columns which flank the door to the other clock. The feet are somewhat heavy, the kidney-shaped door has no inner border and the moldings are crude compared with the Wood clock.

BEST

Mahogany inlaid shelf clock with pewter gilded fretwork, by David Wood, Newburyport, Mass., circa 1790. A masterpiece which exhibits perfection of form and detail. The pewter fretwork is possibly unique and very effective. The ogee bracket feet are of appealing size and form. The value of this clock is many times that of the Boynton clock.

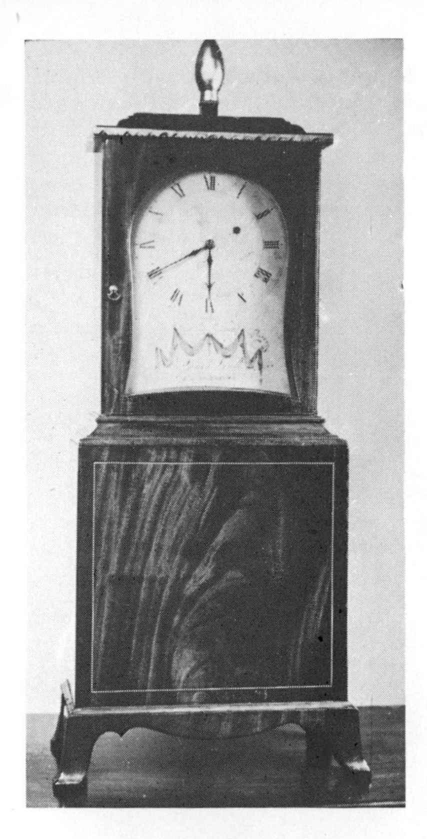

BETTER

Mahogany inlaid shelf clock with kidney-shaped dial, by James South, Charlestown, Mass., circa 1790-1800. An example of fine quality, with the semicircular inlay generally ascribed to John Seymour, the renowned Boston cabinetmaker. The plinth for the center finial protrudes abruptly from the crest, and this can be criticized. Note the beautiful compensating fretwork of the clock shown at bottom of page.

BEST

Mahogany inlaid shelf clock with kidney-shaped dial, by Daniel Munroe, Boston, circa 1790-1800. An American classic of unique design. The fretwork gallery is an inspired variation from the conventional. The superiority of this clock to the one shown at left on facing page is especially evident in the base.

BEST

Mahogany inlaid shelf clock with kidney-shaped dial, by Elnathan Taber, Roxbury, Mass., circa 1780-1800. The crowning masterpiece of this type. The name of the maker is proudly framed by beautiful painted draperies. The background under the dial is a sky-blue color. Courtesy of Museum of Fine Arts, Boston, M. & M. Karolik Collection.

BEST

Miniature hanging wall clock with original glass painting, by David Brown, Providence, R. I., circa 1800-1810. A unique clock of great rarity and desirability. The total length is nineteen inches. The painted glass panel depicts Justice holding the shield bearing the coat of arms of the newly formed United States.

BEST

Mahogany hanging wall clock, by Simon Willard, Roxbury, Mass., circa 1780-1790. This diminutive wall clock is one of the rarest and most important American clocks and is very probably the forerunner of the banjo clock. Unfortunately for those enthusiasts who would give a king's ransom for such an appealing specimen, Simon made very few such clocks.

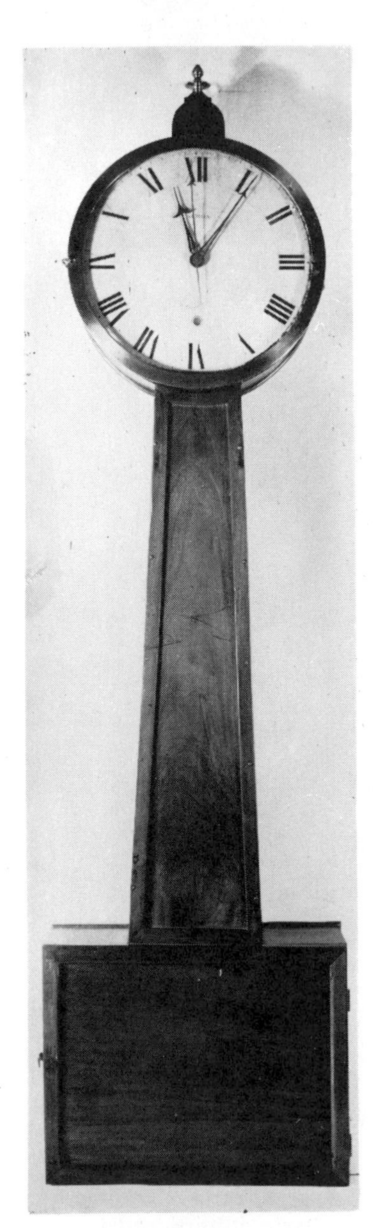

GOOD

Banjo clock, by Simon Willard, Boston, Mass., circa 1800-1810. It is not known whether this clock preceded or anteceded Simon's finest banjo clocks, but in either case it is not successful or beautiful, therefore it cannot be as valuable. It proves that even a great craftsman can make a mediocre specimen now and then.

BEST

Banjo clock with cross-banded borders and the original painted glass panels, by Simon Willard, Boston, circa 1800-1810. One of the finest Simon Willard banjo clocks in existence. Simon invented the banjo clock and patented it in 1802. However, his patent was infringed extensively even by his brothers. Simon's accredited clocks have the white background and "S. Willard's Patent" inscribed on the bottom panel. Simon's designs were generally more restrained than his brother Aaron's; the spread eagle surmounting an atlas in the bottom panel is rare and beautiful.

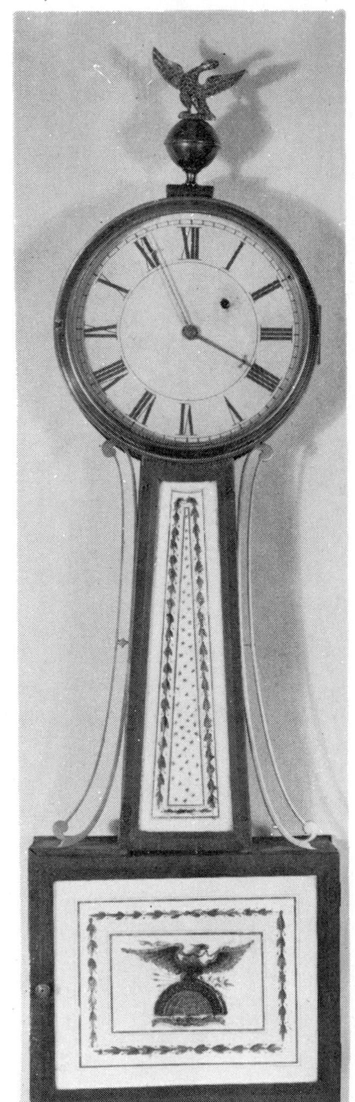

BEST

Banjo clock with cross-banded borders and original glass paintings, by Simon Willard, Boston, Mass., circa 1800-1810. If Simon Willard had left just this one banjo clock to posterity, his fame would be assured. Its beauty of form and design is evident enough, but the outstanding blue borders contrasting with the gilt flowers and white background must be seen to be appreciated.

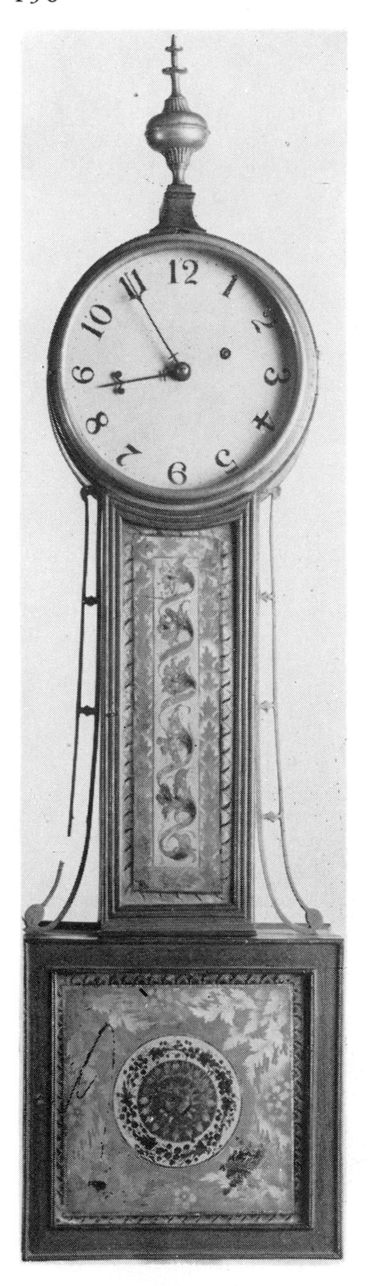

GOOD

Banjo clock with original glass paintings, Boston or vicinity, circa 1810-1820. A clumsy example of little value despite its originality. The beauty of the tapering waist and the rectangular base of the conventional Willard banjo is pointed up by the boxy appearance of this poor example.

BEST

Banjo clock with original glass paintings, by Aaron Willard, Boston, circa 1810-1820. The view of Harvard College depicted on the lower panel makes this a rare example.

BEST

Banjo clock with original glass paintings and gilt spiral borders, by Aaron Willard, Jr., circa 1815. Perhaps the finest quality paintings on any banjo clock. The lower panel depicts the naval engagement between the **Hornet** and the **Peacock** in the War of 1812. The background of the paintings is yellow and the contrasting colors are very effective.

BEST

Girandole clock with original glass paintings, by Lemuel Curtis, Concord, Mass., circa 1810-1820. A great masterpiece which developed from the smaller banjo clock. The value of this great creation by Curtis is enhanced by the fact that less than a handful have survived intact. The bottom panel is convex; this one depicts a Biblical scene. The upper panel has the American shield flanked by the figures of Peace and Justice. The distinctive hands are another mark of this distinctive artisan. This American classic is in a private collection.

The brass works, disassembled hands and winding key of the girandole clock. This illustration affords a view of the brass works, which vary but little from the standard banjo works. Note that the pulley wheel is engraved.

BEST

Lighthouse clock, by Simon Willard, circa 1810-1820. This remarkable type was invented and patented by the versatile Simon Willard. The glass enclosure was probably made in the Sandwich glass factory.

BEST

Lighthouse clock, by Simon Willard, circa 1810-1820. A beautiful example with an octagonal base. Very few of this type clock have survived. They are quite valuable.

GOOD

Pine schoolmaster's desk, New England, circa 1680-1710. A farmhouse piece shown as an example of a class of "Pilgrim" furniture which is revered by those who mistakenly conceive our early culture to be as crude as this piece. Many desks, produced in the same locality during the same era, belie this conception. Such crude work appealed as little to the cultured Pilgrim as it does to today's sophisticated collector.

BETTER

William and Mary maple desk with ball feet, New England, circa 1680-1710. A fine and rare early desk with the well interior.

BEST

William and Mary desk with ball feet and burl walnut veneered front, New England, circa 1700-1720. An American masterpiece. A desk of this quality was used in one of the finest homes of the period. Note the additional refinement of the interior and the ball feet in comparison with the desk shown at right above.

A closed view of desk shown at left. The few examples which have survived are classed as among the most outstanding creations of that early era. Note the magnificent selection of matched veneers and the star inlay on the lid.

BEST

Pilgrim desk-on-frame, New England, circa 1680-1710. This diminutive masterpiece has every desirable feature one could hope for—rarity of type, fine turnings and trumpet feet, and an exceptionally fine blocked interior.

BEST

Early desk-on-frame, Pennsylvania, circa 1680-1710. A very choice example of a rare type. The turnings are most satisfying. It exemplifies the sturdy character of the Pennsylvania citizen and his desire for fine proportion and detail, which this piece achieves.

GOOD

Queen Anne small desk-on-frame, New England, circa 1720-1740. Of the same general form as the piece shown below, the base exhibits crudities which place it in a considerably lower class. Note the crude scrolling of the apron, the squatty base and the clumsy legs and feet.

BEST

Queen Anne small desk-on-frame, New England, circa 1720-1740. An American classic. The slender, perfectly modeled legs, which are of hardly more than pencil thickness at the ankles, did not withstand 200 years of usage by accident. The walnut selected for the purpose was of the finest quality. The high graceful cabriole legs with the finely scrolled apron form a perfect frame for the compact desk section.

GOOD

Queen Anne m a p l e desk-on-frame, New England, circa 1720-1750. A provincial piece made by a mediocre craftsman, as evidenced by the crudely formed cabriole legs.

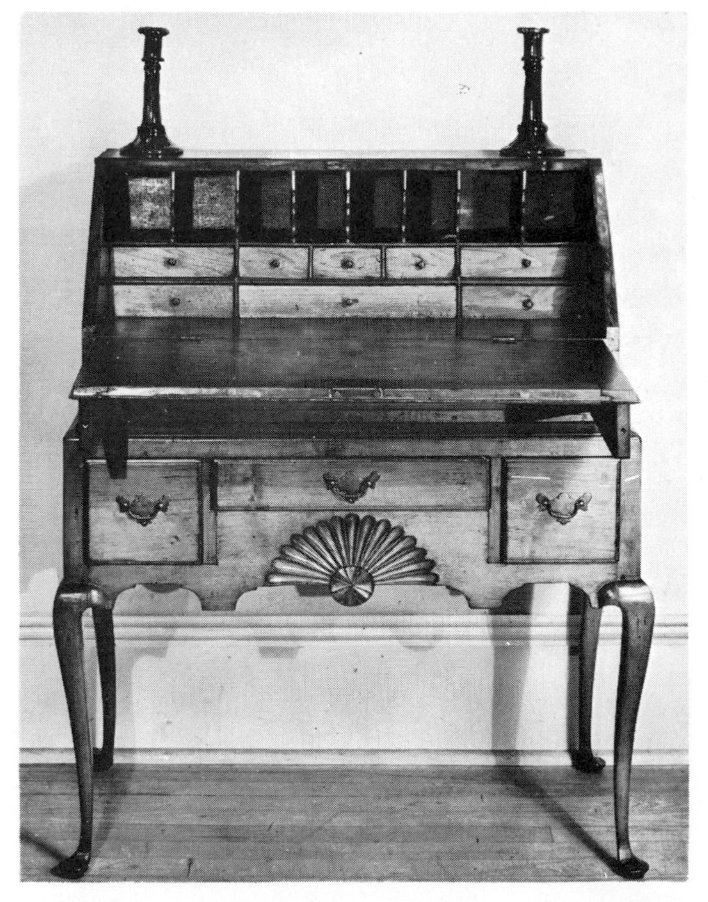

BEST

Queen Anne m a p l e desk-on-frame, New England, circa 1720-1750. A superlative example of a very scarce type, with beautiful cabriole legs and an effective carved fan in the apron.

GOOD

Queen Anne cherry desk with concave blocked interior, Connecticut, circa 1720-1750. A desk of lesser quality than the one shown at bottom of page, but which shows enough affinity to it to assume that the cabinetmaker saw the better desk and tried to emulate it—with only moderate success. Note the crudity of the Queen Anne feet. In the interior, the loss of the second row of drawers is unfortunate from the standpoint of design, as is the extension of the center blocked drawers and pilasters to the fallboard level.

BEST

Queen Anne cherry desk with concave blocked interior, Connecticut, circa 1720-1750. An outstanding desk of desirable small size and exceptional interior of the amphitheater type. Note the fine effects achieved by the double row of blocked drawers and the individualistic scrolling above the pigeonhole compartments. Note that the gracefully curved cabriole legs blend with the body of the piece to form a harmonious unit, while the legs of the piece shown at top of page appear to be disjointed.

BEST

Queen Anne curly maple desk, New England, circa 1720-1750. A choice desk of great rarity. Now in the Edison Institute. The quality is unsurpassed. It is of compact proportions with beautifully shaped cabriole legs and well-defined pad feet. The selection of evenly figured curly maple is remarkable.

GOOD

Chippendale cherry slant-top desk, New England, circa 1750-1780. An average desk of mediocre quality. The bracket feet are crudely formed and the interior is uninspired.

BEST

Chippendale cherry slant-top desk, Connecticut, circa 1750-1780. An American classic, with an exceptional blocked interior, this is certainly one of the finest cherry desks fashioned in the Colonies.

BEST

Chippendale curly maple slant-top desk, New England, circa 1750-1780. A very fine and highly desirable desk with excellent bracket feet and a choice blocked interior. Of the thousands of desks made of native cherry or maple in the eighteenth century only a small minority had interesting interiors. Therefore, an example with an interior of this quality becomes a rarity.

BEST

Chippendale curly maple slant-top desk, Connecticut, circa 1750-1780. One of the great masterpieces of curly maple furniture and a study in bold original design.

Open view of curly maple desk. This outstanding blocked interior is called an "amphitheater" interior because of the effect it creates. It is certainly one of the finest interiors found in a curly maple desk. Note how the small fan in the interior complements the large fan below the lid.

BETTER

Chippendale mahogany desk, Newport, R. I., circa 1750-1780. An excellent comparison of two similar desks whose difference lies mainly in the interior. Probably for reasons of economy, this craftsman left out the three carved fans, scrolling of the pigeonhole brackets and the blocked molding conforming to the shape of the lower drawers. This desk is less valuable than the example illustrated below, just as it was less expensive in the eighteenth century.

BEST

Chippendale mahogany desk, attributed to John Goddard, Newport, R. I., circa 1750-1780. A number of similar desks were made for some of the more prominent citizens of Newport who were willing to pay for a fine interior such as this. The scrolled pigeonhole brackets form six small "secret" drawers. A desk with this quality interior is more valuable than a serpentine-front desk with a plain interior.

BETTER

Chippendale mahogany serpentine-front desk, New England, circa 1750-1780. Many of these desks were made throughout New England, and the exteriors are uniformly excellent. The majority, inexplicably, had plain interiors, so that they are not greatly prized.

BEST

Chippendale mahogany serpentine-front desk, New England, circa 1750-1780. A superlative interior which causes this desk to stand out among examples of its type. The expertly carved fans with the scrolled bases that surmount each pigeonhole serve as the fronts of small pull-out drawers. The finely modeled flame pilasters flanking the center door serve as the fronts of letter compartments. The carved fan in the apron repeats the motif used in the pigeonhole drawers.

BEST

Chippendale mahogany serpentine-front desk, made by Stone and Alexander, Boston, Mass., circa 1760-1780. A desk of exceptional quality. Note especially the superb figured mahogany in the lid and drawers. The latter were hewn from logs at least four inches thick.

Stone *and* Alexander,
Cabinet and *Chair Makers*,
Makes Tables of all kinds,
In the newest Faſhion,
Cornices, Deſks, Book Caſes, Mahogany Chairs,
Sofas, Lolling & eaſy Chairs, &c.
Printed by N. Coverly.

Label in drawer of Stone and Alexander desk. It is unfortunate that so few great craftsmen left their mark on their creations as did these excellent cabinetmakers. A label found on a piece of this quality assumes importance because it identifies a fine craftsman. A maker's name on a mediocre piece increases the value little if any.

BETTER

Chippendale mahogany block-front desk, New England, circa 1750-1780. There was very little inferior block-front furniture, because the effort required to fashion it was too great. It is unusual to be able to offer a contrast as striking as this, for while this desk is of average quality with a plain interior, the example shown below is of exceptional quality even for block-front furniture.

BEST

Chippendale mahogany block-front desk, New England, circa 1750-1780. A superlative example with an exceptional interior. Note the choice figured mahogany used for the drawer fronts, carved from solid logs. Today a four-inch plank of such mahogany could hardly be found. It would be cut into thin sheets of veneer.

Closed view of center desk. The fine proportions and expert bold blocking are evident in this photograph.

BETTER

Chippendale mahogany block-front desk, New England, circa 1750-1780. A fine representative block-front desk. This fan-carved interior, which would be exceptional in a serpentine-front desk, is conventional in this type.

BEST

Chippendale mahogany block-front desk, New England, circa 1750-1780. The blocking of the lower row of three drawers makes this interior more desirable.

BEST

Chippendale mahogany block-front desk with hairy paw feet, New England, circa 1750-1780. One of the finest block-front desks. Few examples of hairy paw foot pieces exist in American furniture. The interior (not illustrated) is outstanding. Even the brasses are exceptional Courtesy of Museum of Fine Arts, Boston, M. & M. Karolik Collection.

BEST

Chippendale mahogany block-front desk with blocked lid, New England, circa 1750-1780. An American classic that expresses the Yankee character of dignity, vigor and honesty. The blocked lid is carved from one solid plank of select mahogany.

Open view of center desk. Although this outstanding desk is an ambitious undertaking, at least four or five examples are known. It is inferred that they were made in the same shop, for all have the individualistic convex shell and identical interiors. This desk is in a private collection.

BEST

Chippendale mahogany block-front kneehole desk, New England, circa 1750-1780. One of a number of universally admired and consistently excellent examples of New England design. Note the bold round block and the fine paneled cupboard door. In a number of these desks the whole center cupboard, containing shelves, is removable.

BEST

Chippendale mahogany block-front kneehole desk, New England, circa 1750-1780. A choice desk in which three recessed drawers replace the more usual paneled door. Note the select figured mahogany. The conventional scalloped apron in the center conceals a narrow drawer.

BEST

Chippendale mahogany block-front kneehole desk, New England, circa 1750-1780. An outstanding desk because of its gilded fan and large bold brasses. Note how the molded top conforms in shape to the blocked drawers, and has just the right overhang for proper balance.

BEST

Chippendale mahogany block-front kneehole desk, New England, circa 1750-1780. A desk of exceptionally fine proportions achieved by the bold narrow square-blocked drawers. In a private collection.

BEST

Chippendale mahogany block-front kneehole desk with carved shells, labeled Edmund Townsend, Newport, R. I., circa 1760-1775. The height of achievement of American craftsmanship and design, rivaled only by the Newport secretary bookcase (page 158) and the Philadelphia highboy (page 188) and lowboy (page 199). This masterpiece of Newport craftsmanship would have been attributed to John Goddard if the label did not add another unknown craftsman to the ranks of the Newport great. Note that with all the details—such as the blocked drawer fronts, the shells, the raised beading on the ogee bracket feet—not one part stands out from the others, but the piece stands as a harmonious, compact unit. Here was no careless assembly or overambitious production; every detail of the original design was carefully planned and more carefully executed. The selection of superlative solid figured mahogany conforms to the quality of the desk. Courtesy of Museum of Fine Arts, Boston, M. & M. Karolik Collection.

Detail of top drawer of Townsend desk. The convex blocked shells are carved from solid blocks of mahogany, then glued to the drawer fronts. They are breathtaking in their scope, their strength and superb execution.

GOOD

Sheraton cherry tambour desk with three drawers, New England, circa 1800. A crude example with poorly shaped apron and turned legs.

BETTER

Hepplewhite mahogany inlaid tambour desk with three drawers, New England, circa 1780-1800. This is a better desk than the one shown at top left and was undoubtedly made by a better craftsman, but the proportion is heavy and clumsy. The legs are too short for the bulk and the top section looks top-heavy.

BEST

Hepplewhite satinwood tambour desk with three drawers, by John Seymour, Boston, Mass., circa 1780-1800. This masterpiece is one of the few specimens of American furniture made entirely of satinwood. It shows the hand of the gifted craftsman and brilliant designer. The tambour slides consist of alternating bands of contrasting woods, a favorite device of John Seymour. The graceful proportions can be better appreciated by noting the difficulty the three other craftsmen had in attempting to master the problem of bulk which is inherent in this type of piece.

BEST

Hepplewhite mahogany inlaid tambour desk with three drawers, New England, circa 1780-1800. A fine example which overcomes the weakness in proportion of the piece shown just above. Actually, from the standpoint of design, the two- or one-drawer tambour desks were more graceful, and most of the *best* examples were made in that form.

BETTER

Hepplewhite mahogany four-drawer tambour desk, New England, circa 1780-1800. A small-sized example of fine quality.

BEST

Hepplewhite mahogany four-drawer tambour desk with satinwood front, Salem, Mass., circa 1780-1800. One of the great masterpieces of the Salem school of satinwood and probably the only example with a three-panel satinwood front. The quality is unsurpassed.

GOOD

Hepplewhite cherry inlaid two-drawer tambour desk, New England, circa 1780-1800. An inferior interpretation of the same general form as that of the desk shown below. The inlay is overdone and not properly placed; the shaped apron adds nothing to the lines and should have been eliminated. The tambour slides themselves are heavy and crude. A claim might be made for this piece that tambour desks of this type are exceedingly rare in cherry. That is true—very few were made in this wood. Still, this desk would bring little on the open market, certainly not a tenth of the price of the other desk.

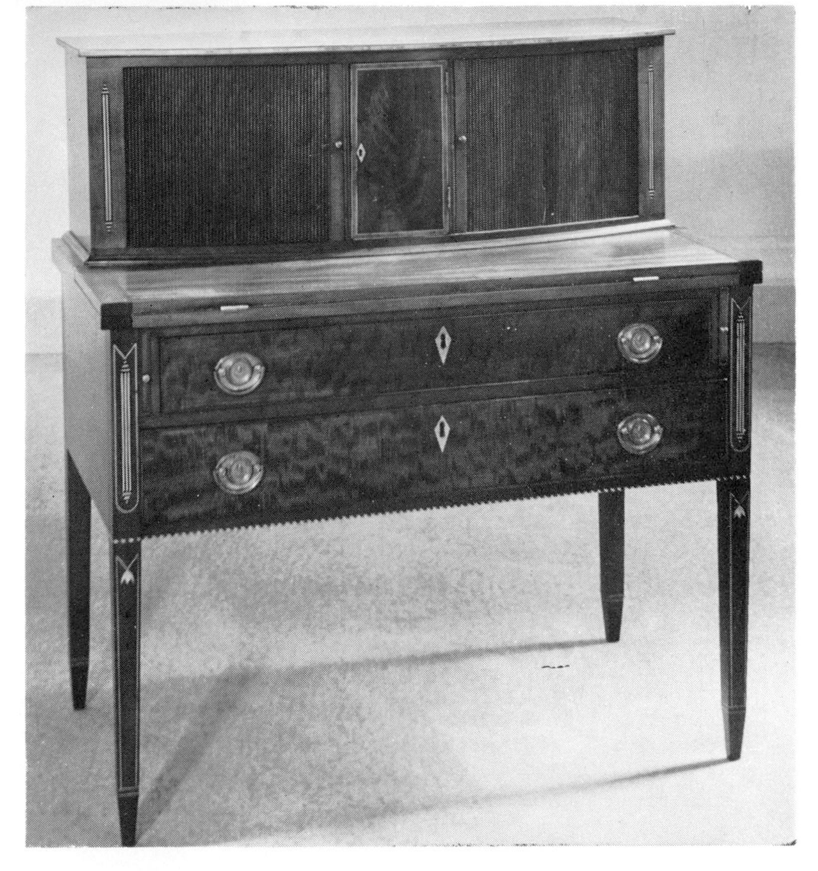

BEST

Hepplewhite mahogany inlaid two-drawer tambour desk, New England, circa 1780-1800. Now in the Edison Institute. One of the outstanding desks of this type because of its superlative quality and fine proportion. The mottled mahogany veneer is exceptional and the extra taper to the base of the leg adds to the delicacy. The tambour section has a gently curved front, a rare feature, especially on a desk of this quality.

BEST

Hepplewhite mahogany inlaid two-drawer tambour desk, attributed to John Seymour, Boston, Mass., circa 1780-1800. At least three of these masterpieces are known, and are ascribed to John Seymour on the basis of a labeled example by that maker. The bellflower inlay on the tambour slides is an achievement in beauty and in execution. This piece is in the Edison Institute.

BEST

Hepplewhite mahogany inlaid two-drawer tambour desk, Salem, Mass., circa 1780-1800. A very choice, delicate example with effective bellflower inlay.

BEST

Hepplewhite mahogany inlaid one-drawer tambour desk, attributed to John Seymour, Charlestown, Mass., circa 1780. A masterpiece of great delicacy and charm, in which the desire for slenderness conquered the usually impelling demands for additional drawer space.

BETTER

Left. William and Mary walnut secretary with ball feet, Salem, circa 1700-1720. Now in the Essex Institute. The paneled doors and lid of this rare secretary indicate an association with the one shown in center. The top is not as fully developed.

BEST

Left center. William and Mary walnut secretary with ball feet, Salem, circa 1700-1720. Few secretary desks were made in this early period, and one of this sophistication is possibly unique. Its tall slender proportions and fine bonnet top are admirable. The star inlay depicts the points of the compass and shows the dominance of commerce in Salem even during that early period. The brass H hinges of the upper doors are engraved as are the escutcheons and plates. This superlative secretary is now in a private collection.

Right center. Interior of secretary at left. The intricate design of the upper and lower interior suggests its use by an influential and busy shipping magnate of that day.

BEST

Right. Queen Anne walnut secretary with bracket feet, Salem, circa 1720-1730. One of the great masterpieces of Early American furniture, this secretary was probably made by the same Salem craftsman as the two other examples on this page, but at the full development of his career. It is slightly less than 30 inches in width and 7 feet 4½ inches high, and brings into focus the desire of Americans to break away from the broad, heavy proportions of contemporary English furniture. Meyric Rogers, curator of the Chicago Art Institute, has developed the logical thesis that the essential difference between American and English design was that the Americans emphasized the vertical while the English favored the horizontal proportion. The American development of the bonnet and broken arch top is an important proof of this contention. Courtesy of Museum of Fine Arts, Boston, M. & M. Karolik Collection.

BEST

Chippendale mahogany secretary, by John Goddard, Newport R. I., circa 1750-1755. An early example by the most famous Newport craftsman. The attribution is based on the carved swans with the ivory eyes forming the front of the pull-out slides. This feature is found on a desk with John Goddard's signature and the date 1754. Note the slender proportions and the well-developed bonnet with the typical blocked hood.

Interior of secretary at top left. The carved shell in the center door is Goddard's trademark and is the same shell later employed on his block-front pieces. The upper interior is very effective.

BEST

Chippendale mahogany block-front six-shell secretary by John Goddard, Newport, R. I., circa 1760-1775. The ultimate in an American secretary and one of the most important pieces of American design and craftsmanship. The development from the earlier secretary (shown above) is apparent. The same blocked shell appears on the center door of the interior of each of the two pieces. Courtesy of Museum of Fine Arts, Boston, M. & M. Karolik Collection.

BETTER

Chippendale mahogany block-front secretary with arched panel doors, New England, circa 1750-1780. The bonnet of the piece is weak and the horizontal molding above the doors would have been better eliminated.

BEST

Chippendale mahogany block-front secretary with arched panel doors, attributed to Benjamin Frothingham, Charlestown, Mass., circa 1750-1780. The superior treatment of the bonnet and the arched panels affords an excellent contrast to the contemporary secretary shown at top of page. This great piece has the sturdy character and vigor which epitomized our New England ancestors.

Interior of Frothingham secretary. An outstanding interior. The carved fans in the top are rare and effective. This secretary is now in a private collection.

GOOD

Chippendale mahogany secretary with arched paneled doors, New England, circa 1750-1780. A mediocre secretary, shown primarily for comparison of the upper section with the one shown below. Notice how the similarly shaped paneling loses effect by its additional width and also by the fact that the top of the door does not follow the contour of the arch. The bonnet also is more cramped.

BEST

Chippendale mahogany block - front secretary with arched paneled doors, New England, circa 1750-1780. This example has the slenderness and height to make it one of the best-proportioned secretaries of the block-front school. Note the perfect formation of the broken arch top. This secretary was discovered intact with the original hardware and flame finials. It is now in a private collection.

Interior of block-front secretary. The many scrolled pigeonholes add beauty and usefulness to this pleasing interior. The concave carved fans in top are found only in the better secretaries of the period.

GOOD

Chippendale mahogany bombé-front secretary, New England, circa 1750-1780. The massive base and small top are definitely out of proportion, resulting in a thoroughly undesirable example of an important type.

Open view of Pepperill secretary. The perfection of line is matched by the excellence of detail in the interior.

BEST

Chippendale mahogany bombé-front secretary, New England, circa 1750-1780. This notable secretary was made for Sir William Pepperill, the hero of the Battle of Louisburg in the French and Indian Wars. He was one of the most prosperous of the New England merchants, and this secretary was naturally fashioned by the best craftsman available. The genius of the cabinetmaker is apparent when we realize he achieved grace and balance in a type piece which, in less expert hands, could easily have appeared ponderous.

GOOD

Chippendale cherry secretary, American, circa 1750-1780. The one thing this inferior secretary has in common with the one shown at bottom of page is scalloped doors of similar general contour; but they are not as bold and are too high for their width.

BEST

Chippendale mahogany serpentine-front secretary with claw and ball feet, New England, circa 1750-1780. The outstanding quality of this choice secretary makes it one of the best of its type. Note the magnificent figured solid mahogany used throughout, also the fine and rare fretwork above the doors. The carved pinwheel in the apron is an effective device.

BEST

Chippendale curly maple serpentine-front secretary with claw and ball feet, by Walter Edge, Gilmantown, N. H., 1799. One of two or three known secretaries of this quality in curly maple. Fortunately, the craftsman signed his name and the date on the back of this secretary in bold contemporary script. The date shows the tendency in rural communities to continue the styles which had gone out of fashion in the large cities. The rarity of this secretary is largely due to the fact that the smaller communities seldom had a craftsman as gifted as this one, and consequently few pieces fashioned from local native woods, such as curly maple, were as fine as this secretary. Note the fine scalloped door panels and the well-defined claw and ball feet.

GOOD

Chippendale mahogany secretary with carved fan in crest, American, circa 1750-1780. The crudity of the embryonic claw and ball feet is immediately apparent. The bonnet is decidedly cramped, with too little open space under the arch. The rectangular paneled doors and the simple interior are far less interesting than those of the masterpiece shown below.

BEST

Chippendale mahogany secretary with carved fan in bonnet and claw and ball feet, New England, circa 1750-1780. One of the finest secretaries produced in the colonies, this beautifully proportioned piece has a remarkably developed interior. Fortunately, the numerous carved fans are expertly done and well spaced.

Closed view of center secretary. The blocked lid is carved from one solid piece of mahogany. The serpentine drawer fronts are likewise. With all its detail, each part blends with the others to form a harmonious unit. This is the acid test which each piece claiming greatness has to pass, whether the elaborations are few or many.

GOOD

Chippendale cherry secretary with broken arch top, Connecticut, circa 1750-1780. Made by a mediocre Connecticut craftsman, this piece exhibits none of the refinements of proportion or detail found in the Chapin secretary.

BEST

Chippendale cherry secretary with broken arch top, by Eliphalet Chapin, Conn., circa 1760-1780. Originally owned by Governor Caleb Strong of Northhampton, Massachusetts. The fine fretwork top is typical of both Aaron and Eliphalet Chapin, who are both recognized as among the foremost cabinetmakers in the Connecticut colony. The quarter columns with the brass stop flutes are effective.

BETTER

Chippendale walnut secretary with **broken arch top, Philadelphia, circa 1750-1780.** A well-proportioned piece which seems to beg for the fine paneled doors of the piece illustrated below.

Interior of Gulick secretary. This desirable blocked interior is found with slight variations in a few of the best desks and secretaries produced in Philadelphia and vicinity.

BEST

Chippendale walnut secretary with broken arch top, Philadelphia, circa 1750-1780. This great classic was made for the Gulick family of Princeton, New Jersey, and always stood in the same house. The deep carved shell is well placed and of superb quality, as are the carved rosettes and flame finials. This piece is now in a private collection.

GOOD

Hepplewhite mahogany secretary with diamond doors, New England, circa 1780-1800. A piece of fine quality, but it appears boxy because of its flat top. The shaped crests of the secretaries shown below show a definite improvement in design.

BEST

Hepplewhite mahogany secretary with diamond doors, New England, circa 1780-1800. A first-quality secretary of fine design and excellent workmanship. The dentil molding at the top and the oval panel in the top drawer are effective refinements. The arched crest with the brass finials adds to the symmetry of the piece.

BEST

Hepplewhite mahogany secretary with diamond doors and satinwood drawer fronts, Salem, Mass., circa 1780-1800. A superlative example of Salem craftsmanship showing the use of the finely figured flame satinwood used extensively during this period by the best Salem and Boston craftsmen.

GOOD

Hepplewhite mahogany tambour secretary, New England, circa 1780-1800. A clumsy piece. The top has too much height in relation to the desk section. The workmanship is good, but not comparable to that of the piece shown in center.

BEST

Hepplewhite mahogany tambour secretary with satinwood fronts, Salem, Mass., circa 1780-1800. A beautifully proportioned specimen with effective use of well-placed flame satinwood. One of the outstanding secretaries of its type.

BEST

Hepplewhite mahogany tambour secretary, attributed to John Seymour, Charlestown, Mass., circa 1780-1800. A masterpiece of fine form and superlative restrained detail. The interrupted tambour slides and the satinwood flanking pilasters were favorite devices of Seymour. The inlaid design of the doors is strikingly beautiful.

GOOD

Left. Hepplewhite mahogany tambour secretary with square tapered legs, Salem, Mass., circa 1780-1800. A piece of important type, but of lesser quality than the example to the right. The top section somewhat overwhelms the lower desk section, and the crest is relatively crude. While this piece could be improved greatly by careful repairing and polishing it could never approach the other secretary in importance or beauty.

BEST

Right. Hepplewhite mahogany tambour secretary with square tapered legs and spade feet, by John Seymour, Charlestown, Mass., circa 1780-1800. One of the great masterpieces of the cabinetmaker's art from every standpoint. The superb proportions are achieved by the proper graduation and size of each of the three sections. The urn-shaped ivory keyhole escutcheons, the interrupted satinwood tambour slides and the cross-banding borders are identifying marks of John Seymour. Every superb detail is integrated into the general pattern.

BETTER

Sheraton mahogany secretary with satinwood fronts, Salem, Mass., circa 1800. A piece of fine workmanship and of an important school, but one which is unsuccessful because the upper and lower parts are not balanced in relation to one another. The top is definitely too low for the size of the base.

BEST

Sheraton mahogany secretary with satinwood fronts, Salem, Mass., circa 1800. A masterpiece of the Salem satinwood school which overcomes the failings of the above example. The detail of the inlaid cross-banded borders is exceptionally beautiful and effective. The legs are more expertly turned than in the other piece.

GOOD

Left. Sheraton mahogany secretary with turned legs, New England, circa 1800. A clumsy, boxy specimen. The base is too wide for proper proportions. The rectangular glass panels are unimaginative.

BETTER

Right. Sheraton mahogany secretary with turned and reeded legs, New York, circa 1820. A clumsy piece of poor proportion. The brilliantly figured mahogany veneer cannot save the piece from mediocrity.

BETTER

Sheraton mahogany and satinwood secretary with turned legs, Salem, Mass., circa 1800-1820. A piece of better proportion and design than either of the two secretaries shown above. The base is more compressed; the treatment of the arched crest and the glass door borders is more effective than that of the secretary shown at right above. The reeded columns flanking the drawers are somewhat heavy. The mahogany center panel on each of th drawers appears unfinished. It should have had a third satinwood panel or had mahogany all the way across.

BEST

Sheraton mahogany secretary with turned and reeded legs, Salem, Mass., circa 1800. A piece of superb and slender proportions and effective restrained detail. Note the beading of the border in the Gothic-shaped doors, also the inlaid platforms on which the vertical columns rest. The legs are slender, well shaped and of sufficient height. Note the unusual brass finials.

GOOD

Sheraton mahogany inlaid bookcase, New England, circa 1800. A mediocre example of an important type made by a third-rate craftsman. The crest is not as finely shaped and the glass door moldings are heavier than those in the example shown at bottom of page. The two turned front legs are crude and inadequate from the standpoint of design. The value of this piece is not high in spite of the importance of its type.

BEST

Hepplewhite mahogany bookcase, New York, circa 1780-1800. An American classic of inspired design. The intertwining pattern of the glass doors and the fine carved border of the top cannot fail to excite admiration. The French feet add to the lightness of this bookcase, probably the finest example produced in New York.

BEST

Hepplewhite mahogany inlaid break-front bookcase, attributed to Edmund Johnson, Salem, Mass., circa 1780-1800. A classic of distinctly American design. The proportions and contours are superb and the crest is beautifully formed. The restrained bellflower inlay and the oval bandings are effectively placed. The square tapered legs lend delicacy to a type which often tends to be cumbersome. One of the outstanding examples of American Hepplewhite furniture.

BEST

Sheraton mahogany secretary with painted glass panels, Salem, Mass., circa 1800. An American classic of the Sheraton period, of delicate form and elegant appearance. The painted glass panels in the upper section are exceptional enough in themselves. The spread eagle and shield add to their interest. Courtesy of Museum of Fine Arts, M. & M. Karolik Collection.

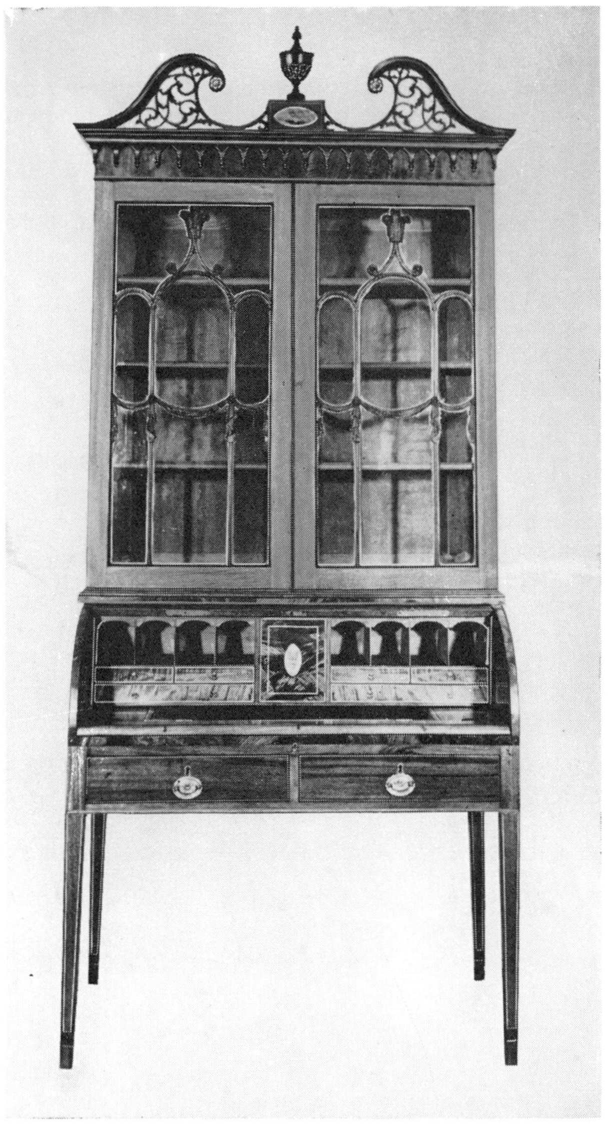

BEST

Hepplewhite mahogany secretary with drapery carved doors, Baltimore, Md., circa 1780-1800. One of the great masterpieces of the Baltimore school. Its slender proportions, fine drapery doors and superlative broken arch top cannot fail to excite the admiration of the most discriminating collector.

Three William and Mary highboys with trumpet legs, New England, circa 1690-1720. Highboys of the quality of any of the following examples of this period which retain the original legs and stretchers are scarce and desirable, since the legs are only doweled into the lower section and the wear of two hundred and fifty years has taken a heavy toll of the underpinnings.

GOOD

Solid walnut front. This artisan erred by making the nicely shaped trumpet too short, giving the leg a spindly appearance.

BETTER

Herringbone walnut veneered fronts. Trumpet legs are stiff and shapeless.

BEST

Beautifully modeled trumpet legs achieve perfect balance. Quite naturally, this fastidious craftsman employed the finest burled veneer fronts.

BETTER

William and Mary highboy with cup turnings, New England, circa 1680-1720. A fine representative maple highboy. However, the turnings lack a crispness and the slenderness apparent in the highboy illustrated below, and the flat stretchers are not as beautifully scrolled.

BEST

William and Mary highboy with cup turnings and burled fronts, New England, circa 1680-1720. A dynamic masterpiece of compact proportions and superlative turnings. The fine burl veneered fronts with the herringbone borders appear on the finest highboys of the period which were made for the most prominent families of that early period; they were the most valuable then as they are now.

BETTER

William and Mary highboy with cup turnings, New England, 1690-1720. Very finely turned legs which cannot be criticized even though they are surpassed by those of the example below. Note how the arch of the apron appears to be sagging while in the other piece the arch is lifted to exalted heights lending additional grace.

BEST

William and Mary highboy with cup turnings, New England, circa 1690-1720. This superlative masterpiece was produced less than one hundred years after the landing of the Pilgrims. It obviously did not repose in a log cabin. The remarkable matched veneers are the natural grain of the crotch section of the tree. Note the satisfying wide flat molding separating the two sections, also the unusual curly maple stretchers and magnificently turned legs. The wide molding at the top conceals a secret drawer. Courtesy of Yale Gallery of Fine Arts.

Two small five-legged highboys, New England, circa 1680-1700. Few examples of this rare type were made and only a handful has survived intact.

BETTER

A country version of great charm, but it lacks the sophistication of the example shown below.

BEST

Superlative example, with the finest turnings. Note the delicacy achieved by the shaped flat stretchers.

BETTER

Early Queen Anne small curly maple highboy with original engraved brasses, New England, circa 1720. Highly desirable example, but not as sophisticated as the piece shown in center.

BEST

Early Queen Anne small highboy with crotch walnut veneered fronts and original engraved brasses, New England, circa 1720. Particularly outstanding because of the graceful cabriole leg and fully developed pad foot. Obviously, the wood selected was thoroughly dried walnut of the finest quality or the slender ankles would have snapped long before this.

BEST

Early Queen Anne small highboy with burled veneer fronts, New England, circa 1720. An American classic of perfect symmetry and superb quality. The engraved brasses are original. The turned finials in the apron are an evolutionary feature—when the two center legs of the William and Mary period were eliminated, these finials took their place. This piece is now in a private collection.

GOOD

Early Queen Anne highboy with crotch walnut veneered fronts, New England, circa 1720. The short stumpy legs and the obvious lack of height of the top section in relation to its width make this a squat, relatively undesirable example of its type.

BEST

Early Queen Anne highboy with crotch walnut veneered fronts, New England, circa 1720. This superior piece corrects every flaw in proportion suffered by the example shown above. The legs have adequate height and a graceful curve. The top section, having sufficient height in relation to the lower section, appears far more slender than the other highboy, although their actual widths probably are the same.

GOOD

Queen Anne curly maple highboy, New England, circa 1740-1760. An average example with an uninteresting base.

BEST

Queen Anne curly maple highboy, New England, circa 1740-1760. A very choice example with an exceptionally fine carved center shell.

BEST

Queen Anne curly maple highboy, New England, circa 1740-1760. A beautifully proportioned example with fine cabriole legs and finely carved fan.

BEST

Queen Anne curly maple highboy, Pennsylvania, circa 1740-1760. A choice highboy of fine proportions. The molded collar above the Spanish foot is typical of the Pennsylvania school.

BEST

Maple highboy, by Dunlap of Concord, New Hampshire, circa 1760. Probably this craftsman's crowning achievement. Several highboys are known by this maker, all having the same effective treatment of the apron and the distinctive fretwork top. The carved rosettes appearing above the fans in the cornice are an unusual touch.

GOOD

Queen Anne maple highboy with bonnet top, New England, circa 1720-1750. A crude country highboy of little merit or charm.

BEST

Queen Anne curly maple highboy with bonnet top, New England, circa 1720-1750. One of the great pieces fashioned of native curly maple, this successful original creation shows what an inspired artist was able to develop from the same general form as that of the piece shown above.

GOOD

A maple bonnet-top example which is illustrated only to show the cramped bonnet and the vast plain surface above the drawers (which prompted Goddard, the perfectionist, to superimpose his raised panels, so notably executed on the example shown at bottom of page). Note the especially clumsy legs of this piece. A medium-quality flat-top highboy would be preferable to this.

BETTER

Queen Anne mahogany bonnet-top highboy with slipper feet, Newport, R. I., circa 1740-1760. A relatively poor example of the same type as that of the one shown below, with fat knees abruptly tapering into too thin ankles.

BEST

Queen Anne mahogany bonnet-top highboy with slipper feet, Newport, R. I., circa 1740-1760, attributed to John Goddard. A beautifully proportioned example with graceful, well-formed cabriole legs. The two raised panels above the drawers are found in many highboys by Goddard and Townsend. Their purpose is solely for design, to help the bonnet-top blend in more harmoniously with the rest of the piece. That they do so is pointed up by their absence on the example shown at top of page.

BEST

Chippendale mahogany bonnet-top highboy, by John Goddard, Newport, R. I., circa 1750-1780. An important example of vigorous lines and masculine character. The original open brasses are exceptional. It is interesting to note that of the several highboys known of this type, no two are alike in treatment of detail, giving each its own individual character and charm.

BEST

A great masterpiece of American design by the superb craftsman, John Goddard, fashioned in Newport, circa 1750-1780. The combination of claw and ball feet in front and pad feet in back is typical of the Newport school, and shows how impossible it often is and how unnecessary to draw a sharp line between periods in the eighteenth century. The blocked bonnet, the fine fluted finials, the carved shell in the apron and the open claw foot are all innovations of the great John Goddard, and are effectively combined in this piece. Courtesy of Museum of Fine Arts, Boston, M. & M. Karolik Collection.

GOOD

Queen Anne bonnet-top highboy, New England, circa 1740. A clumsy bonnet-top highboy with oversized fans, overcurved legs and underdeveloped bonnet.

BEST

Cherry bonnet-top highboy, made in Connecticut by John Brooks in 1769. The bonnet top is one of the most difficult designs to execute successfully, and this is one of the most successful interpretations. The rarity of this superb highboy lies in its quality rather than in its kind, since the highboy illustrated above is of a similar type but is worth scarcely a tenth of the price of this example.

BEST

Queen Anne curly walnut bonnet-top highboy, by Benjamin Frothingham, Charlestown, Mass., circa 1740-1760. A superlative specimen by a craftsman who was a major during the Revolution and a friend of Washington's. The proportions and quality are admirable and the curly walnut selected is of the utmost rarity. Note how the curve of the top end drawers conforms to the shape of the bonnet.

BEST

Queen Anne mahogany bonnet-top highboy with cushioned pad feet, New England, circa 1740-1760. A choice highboy of exceptional quality and importance. The bonnet-top highboy was created in this country by our Colonial craftsmen. Examples such as this have made it recognized as an important contribution to furniture design. The ratio of the width to the height results in a slender appearance, which is heightened by the well-shaped bonnet and the finely curved cabriole legs. Note the quality of the carved fan and the spiral finials.

GOOD

Chippendale scroll-top highboy, Philadelphia, circa 1750-1780. A cumbersome example of a very important type. It suffers from too deep a lower section, caused by placing two long drawers above the carved shell instead of one.

BETTER

Chippendale scroll-top highboy, Philadelphia, circa 1750-1780. A far better investment, at several times the price of the highboy shown above, solely because of its finer proportions. The placing of the upper shell drawer between the two small drawers instead of above them is a definite improvement, as it allows more open space between the scrolls, making the bonnet appear less cramped.

BEST

Chippendale scroll-top highboy, Philadelphia, circa 1750-1780. Certainly one of the greatest—if not the supreme—of the Philadelphia highboys. Flawless in design and proportion, constructed as a labor of love. The magnificent selection of figured mahogany is, in itself, exceptional. Courtesy of Museum of Fine Arts, Boston, M. & M. Karolik Collection.

GOOD

Chippendale scroll-top highboy, American, circa 1750-1780. A clumsy version of a highboy vaguely similar in type but vastly inferior in quality, proportion and design to the highboy shown below. Undesirable in its present form, this highboy would have been an important example if it had been made by a craftsman with a better knowledge of proportion.

BEST

Chippendale cherry scroll-top highboy, by Eliphalet Chapin, Connecticut, circa 1750-1780. The ultimate achievement in a Connecticut highboy and a study in bold original design and superb proportions. Like any great work of art, each component part flows into the other, blending into a harmonious unit. The craftsmanship and detail are of the highest order.

GOOD

William and Mary lowboy with cup turnings, New England, circa 1690-1720. Fine turnings, but the drawers do not take up enough space, leaving too much room between them and the apron.

BEST

William and Mary lowboy with cup turnings, New England, circa 1690-1720. A lowboy of first quality and excellent turnings.

BEST

William and Mary lowboy with cup turnings, New England, circa 1690-1720. A masterpiece of early furniture, with unique turnings done by a virtuoso with a highly developed sense of balance. Note the effective center finial, the turning of which matches those of the legs.

GOOD

Queen Anne walnut lowboy, New England, circa 1720-1750. Bulky in proportion and not the best-shaped cabriole leg.

BETTER

Queen Anne walnut lowboy, New England, circa 1720-1750. A well-proportioned example with a fine cabriole leg. Note the improvement (over the piece shown above) attained by the more compact body of the piece.

BEST

Queen Anne walnut lowboy, New England, circa 1720-1750. The walnut veneered front and top with its finely figured grain make this graceful lowboy the most important of the three illustrated on this page.

BEST

Queen Anne walnut lowboy, attributed to William Savery, Philadelphia, circa 1720-1750. An outstanding example of fine proportions, with the incised carving on the knees found on one or more labeled Savery pieces.

BEST

Queen Anne lowboy of diminutive size, Connecticut, circa 1720-1750. A dynamic little lowboy with most satisfying proportions and probably unique feet. The product of another individualistic Connecticut craftsman, it would not remain long in any dealer's shop, no matter how remote.

GOOD

Queen Anne walnut lowboy with concave blocked center drawer, Rhode Island, circa 1720-1750. An average lowboy of this type. The proportions and craftsmanship are not as fine as in the example illustrated directly below, and the legs do not have as good a curve.

BEST

Queen Anne walnut lowboy with concave blocked center drawer, Rhode Island, circa 1720-1750. The effective C scrolls on the legs and the unusual side brasses raise this fine lowboy out of the ordinary class.

BEST

Queen Anne walnut lowboy with concave blocked center drawer, Rhode Island, circa 1720-1750. One of the best Rhode Island lowboys. The compact proportions, the deep shell to relieve the plainness of the concave blocking and the walnut veneered fronts help to make this an American classic. It is now in a private collection.

BEST

Queen Anne block-front lowboy, New England, circa 1740-1760. One of the great rarities of the block-front school, this unique and successful lowboy was purchased from Priscilla Alden, a direct descendant of Priscilla Alden of Pilgrim days. It is now in a private collection.

BEST

Queen Anne mahogany lowboy with carved shell in apron, attributed to John Goddard, Newport, R. I., circa 1740-1760. An outstanding example of the Goddard-Townsend school, with the typical Newport shell found in Goddard block-front pieces. By a lucky coincidence, this piece has recently been reunited with its matching highboy and is now in a private collection.

GOOD

Left. A Queen Anne maple lowboy with carved fan, New England, circa 1720-1750. The legs of this otherwise pleasing piece are too stiff and straight for perfect symmetry.

BEST

Below. Queen Anne walnut lowboy, New England, circa 1720-1750. A most attractive lowboy with the inlaid fan and with particularly pleasing lines. Now in a private collection.

BETTER

Queen Anne walnut lowboy, New England, circa 1720-1750. An average example of good quality. One instinctively feels the need of a carved fan in the center drawer, as in the example illustrated below, for it seems to tie the piece together. Since the effectiveness of a carved or inlaid central motif is recognized, a lowboy such as this is not as important as a lowboy of like quality with a fan.

Detail of the carved fan of the lowboy shown below.

BEST

Queen Anne mahogany lowboy, New England, circa 1720-1750. A choice example, the vast improvement effected by the carved fan in the center drawer. The use of mahogany in this period is not common. This lowboy is in daily use in a private home.

GOOD

Queen Anne cherry lowboy, Connecticut, circa 1720-1750. A crude, clumsy version with a thick body and heavy legs. The fan is obviously too small for the drawer, and the craftsman tried unsuccessfully to compensate for it with the two triangular fans in the upper corners.

BETTER

Queen Anne cherry lowboy, Connecticut, circa 1720-1750. A good Connecticut lowboy of unusual height, with the same scalloped apron as on the example shown below, but of lesser importance. Although the quality of the cabriole legs and the scalloped apron is as fine, it is not equal to the other piece from the standpoint of proportion, since it appears spindly by comparison. The carved clover leaf in the center drawer is not as effective as the finely carved fan.

BEST

Queen Anne cherry lowboy, Connecticut, circa 1720-1750. An outstanding lowboy of brilliant design. The rectangular top on a lowboy was too plain for this craftsman, so he shaped it all around to conform to the curves of the apron. It is another example of the refusal of the highly individualistic Connecticut craftsmen to follow the usual New England patterns.

BETTER

Chippendale mahogany lowboy with scalloped apron, New England, circa 1750-1780. A less successful example than the lowboy illustrated below. The top hangs too close to the body and the apron has a weak curve which makes the body appear too fat.

BEST

Chippendale mahogany lowboy with scalloped apron, New England, circa 1750-1780. An outstanding lowboy of dynamic proportions. Note the effectiveness of the bold overhang of the top.

GOOD

Chippendale mahogany lowboy, New England, circa 1750-1780. This craftsman made three mistakes, all of which are avoided in the example illustrated directly below. He made the body too wide, not allowing enough overhang of the top for proper balance. He made the leg too fat below the knee. He put the fan in the center of the drawer so that it looks lost.

BEST

Chippendale mahogany lowboy, New England, circa 1750-1780. A choice example with carved knees. It retains the pad foot in back, a most unusual treatment outside of Newport. This lowboy was probably made in Salem.

BEST

Chippendale mahogany lowboy, New England, circa 1750-1780. The magnificent carved shell in the center drawer as well as the quality of the piece raises this lowboy into the first rank. Its authentic history of descent in the family of John Hancock adds much to its interest as well as to its monetary value. If it were a mediocre piece, the history could do little for it.

BEST

Chippendale walnut lowboy, Philadelphia, circa 1740-1760. A bold little thoroughbred of dynamic proportions. It will surpass in value a carved Philadelphia lowboy of mediocre quality, although it will not equal the value of the lowboy shown below, which contains the carved shell in the center drawer.

Detail of carved shell of lowboy illustrated below. Note the delicacy and grace of the carved vines and the magnificent detail of the shell itself.

BEST

Chippendale walnut lowboy with carved shell in center drawer, Philadelphia, circa 1750-1780. An outstanding example of superb quality, with exceptional openwork brasses. The carved shell and tracery are finer than on most of the more florid examples. Now in a private collection.

GOOD

Chippendale mahogany lowboy Philadelphia, circa 1770. A box on legs. The clumsy proportions and crudely carved shell in the center drawer make this an undesirable piece.

BETTER

Chippendale mahogany lowboy, Philadelphia, circa 1770. The quality of this lowboy is better than that of the piece shown above, but the body is too deep for perfect proportions. This piece lacks the attractive carved vines present on the best lowboys of this type, such as the one illustrated below.

BEST

Chippendale mahogany lowboy, Philadelphia, circa 1770. A masterpiece of Colonial design and craftsmanship. Note how effectively the feeling of heaviness is eliminated by reducing the depth of the body and by making the legs higher.

BEST

Chippendale curly maple lowboy with carved shell in center drawer, Philadelphia, circa 1740-1760. One of the great rarities in curly maple, this lowboy is, to our knowledge, the only known conventional Philadelphia Chippendale lowboy in curly maple. It is now in a private collection.

Detail of carved shell of curly maple lowboy. The boldness of the shell and vines gives a feeling of strength. The softness of the edges through the natural erosion of the atmosphere over two hundred years is apparent in this photograph and is evidence of genuineness in addition to contributing to the mellow beauty of a fine antique piece.

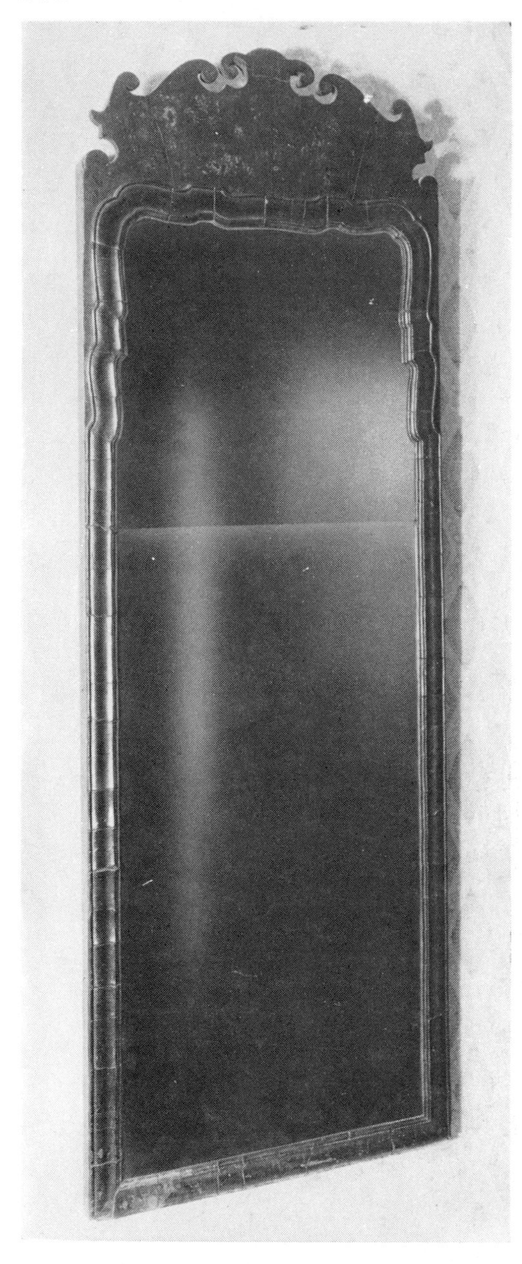

BEST

Queen Anne walnut mirror with original two-section beveled glass, American, circa 1740-1760. A fine conventional mirror. It has a nicely scrolled crest but lacks the carved and gilded shell of the mirror shown at right.

BEST

Queen Anne walnut mirror with original two-section beveled glass, Philadelphia, circa 1740-1760. One of the best mirrors of this type from every standpoint. The superlative gilt shell in the crest is analogous to the carved shell of the Philadelphia lowboy. The bold molding and the incised gilt border are of the highest quality.

BEST

Queen Anne walnut mirror with the original two-section beveled glass, Philadelphia, circa 1740-1760. A superb mirror, with bold moldings and exceptionally finely incised gilt border. The carved and gilded ornament in the crest aids in making this mirror one of the masterpieces of its type.

BEST

Queen Anne walnut mirror with the original two-section beveled glass, Philadelphia, circa 1740-1760. An outstanding and exceedingly rare mirror of the finest quality. The relief carving on the crest is an almost unique feature, bold and beautifully done. This choice mirror is now in a private collection.

GOOD

Queen Anne mirror with the original two-section glass, New England, circa 1740-1760. Note the weak molding and the lack of the incised gilded border.

BEST

Queen Anne walnut mirror with the original two-section beveled glass, New England, circa 1740-1760. An exceptionally fine mirror with carved and gilded side ornaments. The proportions and quality are unsurpassed. Note how the weak elongated effect of the mirror illustrated at left is avoided by means of the side drapes, the shaped molding and the applied ornament on the crest. Courtesy of Museum of Fine Arts, Boston, M. & M. Karolik Collection.

BETTER

Chippendale walnut mirror with gilded shell in crest, Philadelphia, circa 1750-1780. A good representative mirror, but a less ambitious production than the mirror illustrated below. It could have been less broad in relation to its height; the other mirror is a finely proportioned example.

BEST

Chippendale walnut mirror with gilt side draperies, Philadelphia, circa 1750-1780. An exceptional mirror with a rare and well-executed basket-of-fruit ornament. This valuable mirror is in daily use in a private collection.

GOOD

Chippendale mirror, New England, circa 1750-1780. An inferior mirror with crude scrolling and border.

BETTER

Chippendale mirror with carved and gilded phoenix in crest, New England, circa 1750-1780. Although better than the mirror shown at left, it is a poor example, especially when compared with the mirror illustrated below.

BEST

Chippendale mirror with carved and gilded phoenix in crest, New England, circa 1750-1780. Note the well-formed bird, the superior scrolling and the excellent border surrounding the glass. A fine representative mirror.

BETTER

Right. Chippendale mahogany mirror with gilt side draperies, New England, circa 1750-1780. A startling contrast between two mirrors of similar form. The scrolled hood and the phoenix ornament are weak in form and inept in workmanship compared with the mirror illustrated at left—also the gilt side draperies are not as skillfully carved.

BEST

Chippendale mahogany mirror with gilt side draperies, New England, circa 1750-1780. A mirror of this quality is almost impossible to procure in the most desirable state, i.e., with the original side draperies and the original bird ornament. When one does turn up, the wise collector does not pause to dicker but snaps it up as did the fortunate private collector who now owns this example.

BEST

Chippendale mahogany and gilt "Constitution" mirror, American, circa 1750-1780. A fine representative mirror. The superb side pieces in this and mirrors of like quality are carved of wood and then gilded, as are the carved moldings and center ornament. The bird is finely sculptured and is of lifelike appearance.

BEST

Chippendale mahogany mirror with gilt side draperies, New England, circa 1750-1780. An outstanding mirror with fine and unusual pierced scrolling.

BEST

Chippendale mahogany and gilt "Constitution" mirror, American, circa 1750-1780. The principal difference between the American and English mirrors of this period is proportion. The American mirrors tend to have less width and more height—the English are broader. The carved moldings of this mirror are very fine.

BEST

Chippendale mahogany and gilt pier mirror, New England, circa 1750-1780. A choice mirror. It has the finest proportion and quality. Note the natural modeling of the bird ornament. One of the best of the New England mirrors. Courtesy of Museum of Fine Arts, Boston, M. & M. Karolik Collection.

1

BEST

Chippendale mahogany and gilt mirror, New England, circa 1750-1780. An American masterpiece, carved and inspired by genius. One of the truly great American mirrors. The long slender proportions are most satisfying. Note the perfect curve to the broken arch top and the effective scrolled terminals. Courtesy of Museum of Fine Arts, Boston, M. & M. Karolik Collection.

2

BEST

Chippendale mahogany "Constitution" mirror, New York, circa 1750-1780. A striking mirror of fine and unusual design. The egg and dart gilt moldings are effective.

BEST

Chippendale mahogany oval mirror with side draperies, New England, circa 1750-1780. A rare and possibly unique mirror of successful proportions and design.

BETTER

Left. Hepplewhite mahogany inlaid mirror with drapery sides, New York, circa 1780-1800. A fine mirror of excellent proportions. The side draperies, while not too delicately carved, avoid a cumbersome effect.

BEST

Right. Sheraton gilt mirror with painted panel in the crest, depicting George Washington, American, circa 1800. A superlative mirror of the period with the rare and effective employment of the picture of the founder of the new republic. Courtesy of Museum of Fine Arts, Boston, M. & M. Karolik Collection.

BEST

Left. Hepplewhite mahogany inlaid mirror with painted glass panel, New York, circa 1780-1800. One of the best American mirrors of this period, of slender proportions and excellent detail. Note the fine curve to the gilt scrolled top.

BEST

Right. Hepplewhite mahogany inlaid mirror with side leaves, New England, circa 1780. A great masterpiece of superb proportions and exquisite detail. The urn ornament is more fully developed and more finely modeled than are the ornaments on most mirrors.

GOOD

Sheraton gilt mirror with original painted glass panel, New York, circa 1800-1820. A mediocre example with heavy turned columns. It lacks the delicacy that graces the better mirrors of the Sheraton period, such as is apparent in the mirror illustrated directly below.

BEST

Sheraton gilt mirror with original painted glass panel, New England, circa 1800. A fine mirror with effective spiral moldings which effect a light appearance. The painted landscape is attractive.

BEST

Sheraton gilt mirror with original painted glass panel, New England, circa 1800. A finely proportioned mirror. The spread eagle and shield painting, symbolizing, as it does, our newly acquired independence, adds interest and importance to this mirror.

BEST

Sheraton gilt mirror with original painted glass panel, surmounted by spread eagle and urn finials, New York, circa 1800. An outstanding mirror of important design. The urns are better formed than those on mirror illustrated at left, and have attractive sprays. The painted scene is important, showing the American ship in the center, and the quality of the painting itself is high. The vertical columns are slender. Several fine mirrors of this quality were made for the Van Renssalaer and other prominent New York families.

GOOD

Left. Sheraton gilt mirror with original painted glass panel, surmounted by spread eagle and side finials, New York, circa 1800-1820. A clumsy mirror with heavy spiral columns and relatively clumsy eagle and side finials.

GOOD

Sheraton gilt mirror with original ship painting, New England, circa 1800. An inferior mirror with crude moldings. The painted glass panel is too large in relation to the total size of the mirror.

Label on back of mirror illustrated below. A beautifully engraved label. Its importance lies mainly in the fact that it occurs on one of this maker's best productions.

BEST

Sheraton gilt mirror with original ship painting, by John Doggett, Roxbury, Mass., circa 1800. An outstanding mirror by John Doggett, who made Simon Willard's banjo clock cases. Note the improvement in design (as compared with the mirror shown at left above) created by the more compact, painted panel of superior artistry. The painting was undoubtedly done by the same artist who did the painted glass panels for Simon Willard's banjo clocks. The quality of the fluted columns and the Corinthian capitals provides startling contrast to the primitive columns of the other mirror.

GOOD

Gilt convex mirror, American, circa 1800-1820. Just after the turn of the century, the vogue of heavy-line furniture developed, which later degenerated into the massive Empire period. This mirror reflects that tendency, and is far less desirable than those mirrors which retained the Sheraton influence of fine line and delicacy, such as is apparent in the example illustrated at bottom of page.

BETTER

Gilt convex mirror, Albany, N. Y., circa 1800-1820. An interesting mirror of unusual form. The eagle, while fine in itself, appears too heavy for the rest of the mirror.

BEST

Gilt convex mirror, Boston, Mass., circa 1800. A superlative mirror, in which each component part blends into a harmonious whole. Courtesy of Museum of Fine Arts, Boston, M. & M. Karolik Collection.

SIDEBOARDS

GOOD

Hepplewhite mahogany bow-front sideboard, New England, circa 1780. Slightly heavy example of a scarce type. The legs are chunky and do not taper sufficiently at the base. A border of line inlay on the legs with the cross-banded cuffs near the base, as in the example shown below, would have made the legs appear lighter without making the sideboard ornate.

BEST

Hepplewhite mahogany bow-front sideboard, New England, circa 1780. Compact, beautifully proportioned example which cannot fail to excite the most discriminating collector. Note the additional taper at the base of the legs which adds to the delicacy of the piece. The cross-banded borders of the doors and drawers and the fine figured fronts relieve the monotony of large plain surfaces, while avoiding any criticism of flamboyance. The fluted circular brasses are exceptional.

GOOD

Hepplewhite mahogany inlaid sideboard, Virginia, circa 1780. A provincial interpretation of a sideboard, in which the maker attempted to provide a large number of drawers and cupboards.

BEST

Hepplewhite mahogany inlaid sideboard, New England, circa 1780. A highly successful achievement, combining utilitarian and aesthetic functions.

BETTER

Hepplewhite mahogany D-shape sideboard with spade feet, New England, circa 1780. A good representative New England sideboard.

BEST

Hepplewhite mahogany D-shape sideboard with spade feet, New England, circa 1780. A superior interpretation of the same form as that of the piece shown above, and obviously a more expensive product when it was made. The veneered fronts are richer in figure and tone—the diagonal inlaid borders and the center tambour section add lightness and character to this outstanding piece.

BETTER

Hepplewhite mahogany serpentine-front sideboard with fan inlay and inverted cup inlay on legs, New York or New Jersey, circa 1780. A fine representative example of this type, many of which were made for the most prominent New York and New Jersey residents. The end cupboards were made for someone who demanded extra cupboard space.

BEST

Hepplewhite mahogany serpentine-front sideboard with fan inlay and superb octagonal brasses, New England, circa 1780. A choice sideboard of bold contours and restrained detail. The chased octagonal brasses are exceptional. Much of the charm of this sideboard is found in the warm, mellow color which is peculiar to New England pieces that have not been refinished, which a photograph, unfortunately, cannot capture.

BEST

Hepplewhite mahogany serpentine-front sideboard with fan inlay and inverted cup inlay on legs, New York or New Jersey, circa 1780. A superior example of an important type. It is lighter in feeling and better designed than the example illustrated at top of page.

BEST

Hepplewhite mahogany inlaid serpentine-front sideboard, New York, circa 1780. A masterpiece of American design and craftsmanship—one of the great pieces of its period. It stands on high slender legs, like a proud thoroughbred race horse. Its delicacy illustrates the essential difference between American and English sideboards of this period: the American examples have more height in relation to the body and offer a more graceful appearance. Courtesy of Museum of Fine Arts, Boston, M. & M. Karolik Collection.

BEST

Hepplewhite mahogany serpentine-front sideboard, by Mills and Deming, New York, circa 1780. Known as the Wolcott sideboard. One of the great masterpieces of American eighteenth century furniture, now in a private collection. This sideboard was made for Governor Oliver Wolcott, one of the Connecticut signers of the Declaration of Independence. It is fortunate that it retains the label of Mills and Deming, for this piece alone places them among the immortals of furniture craftsmen.

GOOD

Hepplewhite mahogany inlaid serpentine-front sideboard, New York, circa 1780. An above-average sideboard, but it lacks the refinement of the piece shown below both in detail and in grace. The legs do not have the height and delicacy, the edge of the top is relatively crude as is the inlay.

BEST

Hepplewhite mahogany inlaid serpentine-front sideboard, New York, circa 1780. A masterpiece of form and quality. Note the finely matched figured mahogany offset in the circular panels. Also the canted center legs which conform to the serpentine curve.

BETTER

Hepplewhite mahogany serpentine-front sideboard, New England, circa 1780. A well-shaped sideboard with finely figured crotch veneers.

BEST

Hepplewhite mahogany serpentine-front sideboard, New England, circa 1780. A more masterful development of the same general design as the above sideboard. The design of this piece worked a simple but effective circle or oval banding in each drawer and door, thus breaking the monotony of large plain surfaces. To some collectors, the dignity, grace and simplicity of a sideboard such as this represent the acme of design.

GOOD

Hepplewhite four-legged mahogany sideboard, Baltimore, circa 1780. An average example of no particular distinction. The legs are chunky and do not have the height or grace of the legs of the piece shown below. The recessed center section only emphasizes the bulkiness of the rounded ends, while the serpentine center of the other piece creates a harmonious unity.

BEST

Hepplewhite four-legged mahogany sideboard, Baltimore, circa 1780. A very choice example of unusually beautiful proportions. This sideboard is sometimes called "kidney-shaped," and few examples are as successful as this one. The bellflower inlay on the legs and the oval panels above are superb.

BEST

Hepplewhite mahogany serpentine-front sideboard with bellflower inlay, Baltimore, circa 1780. A choice example of pleasing form and superlative inlay. The typical Baltimore bellflower inlay on the legs is contained within an elongated panel of light wood.

BEST

Hepplewhite mahogany double serpentine-front sideboard, Baltimore, circa 1780. A masterpiece of Baltimore craftsmanship. The expert placement of inlay and satinwood panels is matched by the superb proportions and selection of finely matched figured mahogany.

GOOD

Sheraton mahogany server or small sideboard, New York, circa 1800. A unique server, by Duncan Phyfe, which he evidently didn't repeat because it presents too boxy an appearance.

BEST

Hepplewhite mahogany inlaid server, Providence, R. I., circa 1780. A well-balanced, highly desirable server—the product of an individualistic and gifted Rhode Island craftsman. The handful of examples which has turned up show strong evidence of having been made by one man. He avoided by skillful designing the boxy effect of the example shown above. The body is not as deep and the cross-banded borders further lighten the effect. The intersecting inlaid vines are a typical device on this type of server.

BEST

Hepplewhite mahogany server with tambour fronts and spade feet, by the renowned John Seymour, cabinetmaker of Boston, Mass., circa 1780-1800. The masterful interrupted tambour and the scrolled brackets, as well as the inlaid pilasters, are typical devices of Seymour. The quality and proportions of this masterpiece are unsurpassed.

GOOD

Sheraton mahogany shaped sideboard, New York, circa 1800-1820. The cumbersome, clumsy effect of this sideboard is heightened when contrasted to the delicacy of the example illustrated below. The fatness of the reeded legs and the bulk of the body contribute to its heaviness. It begins to show the deterioration in form of the Empire period, which reduced its standing in relation to the earlier periods even though the quality of construction remained high.

BEST

Sheraton mahogany and satinwood bow-front sideboard, New England, circa 1800. There were not many successful sideboards created in this period, since the many beautiful designs of the Hepplewhite sideboards remained popular through most of the Sheraton period. But this example is so exceptional in delicacy and workmanship that it ranks with the finest of the Hepplewhite sideboards.

BEST

Chippendale mahogany camel-back sofa, Philadelphia, circa 1750-1780. A fine example, distinguished by the fish scale carving on the legs.

BEST

Chippendale mahogany camel-back sofa, molded legs with astragal carving, Philadelphia, circa 1750-1780. An outstanding sofa with fine serpentine back and roll arms. The astragal beading in the finely molded legs adds to the desirability of this example. The great demand for this type of American sofa has created a high value on the few surviving examples of this quality.

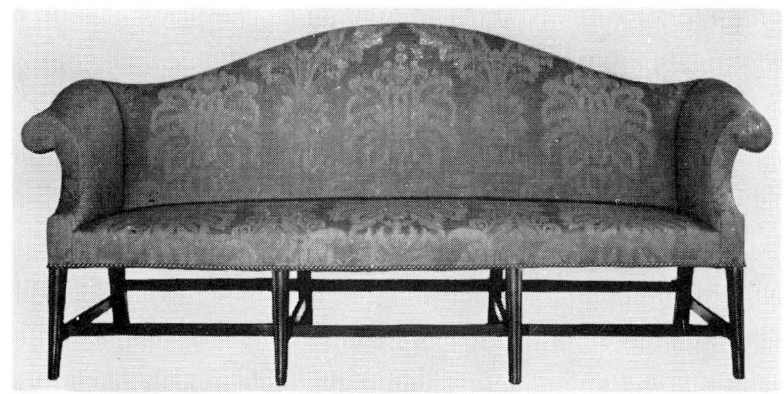

BEST

Chippendale mahogany camel-back sofa with molded legs, New England, circa 1750-1780. A rare type with unusually fine proportions. An exceptionally graceful sofa of small size. One of the best of the few sofas of this period known to have originated in New England. This sofa now graces the living room of a private collector.

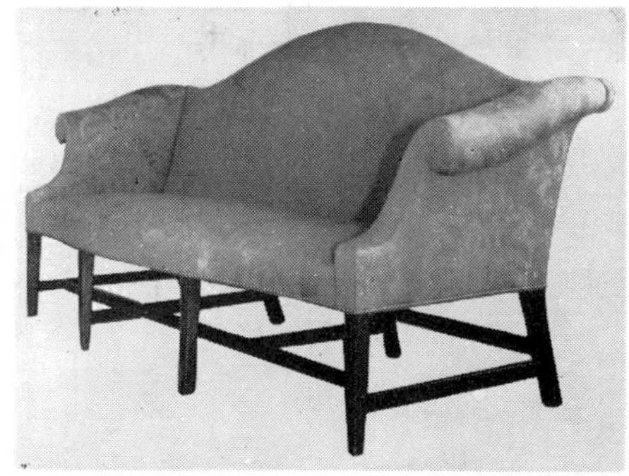

Another view of sofa illustrated at left, showing the serpentine curve of the roll arm.

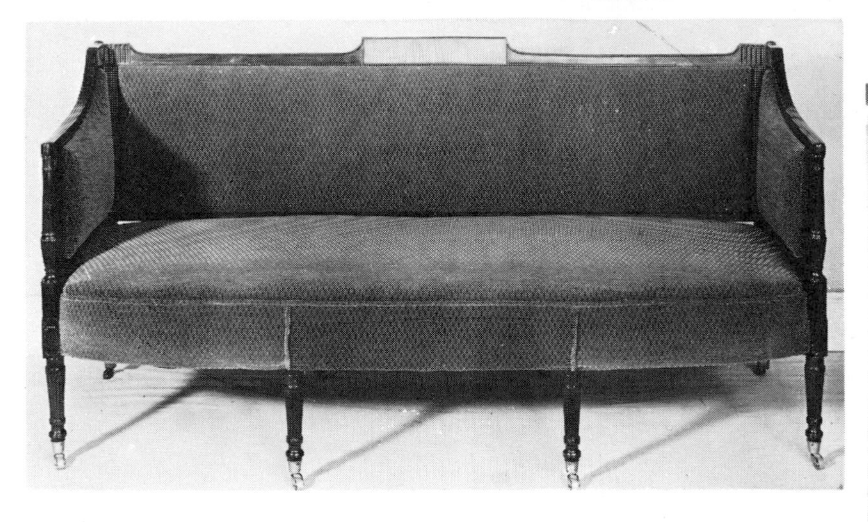

GOOD

Above: Sheraton mahogany sofa with inlaid panel in back, Maryland, circa 1780-1800. An average example of a type which reaches exalted heights in the sofa illustrated below.

Right: Detail of sofa below. The rectangular-shaped panel of inlay identifies the work of a first-class Baltimore craftsman. The expert handling of the intertwining line inlay on the legs conforms with the quality exhibited in every phase of this fine sofa.

BEST

Below: Sheraton mahogany sofa with inlaid panel in back and typical Baltimore inlay on legs, Maryland, circa 1780-1800. The increased height of the center panels of the crest rail affords better balance.

BEST

Hepplewhite mahogany small sofa with bell-flower inlay, Baltimore, circa 1780-1800. In a private collection. One of the few sofas with the bellflower inlay more frequently found in tables and other pieces of the period. The contours are unusual and graceful.

BEST

Sheraton mahogany and satinwood sofa, Salem, Mass., circa 1800. An American classic made to order for General Knox and formerly exhibited in the Knox Museum. It is probably the longest American sofa known, being nine feet in length, and is the highest development of this type of Salem sofa. The slender feeling of a sofa of this size is an achievement.

GOOD

Above. Sheraton mahogany sofa with reeded legs, New England, circa 1800. A mediocre sofa with a stiff straight crest and heavily reeded legs.

BEST

Below. Sheraton mahogany sofa with reeded legs, New England, circa 1800. A choice example with a gently bowed crest. The arms arch gradually into the back, instead of abruptly as in the sofa illustrated at left above.

GOOD

Above. Sheraton mahogany sofa with reeded legs, Salem, Mass., circa 1800. A poorly designed sofa with a stunted straight back and cumbersome arms.

BEST

Below. Sheraton mahogany sofa with reeded legs, Salem, Mass., circa 1800. A choice example of perfect symmetry.

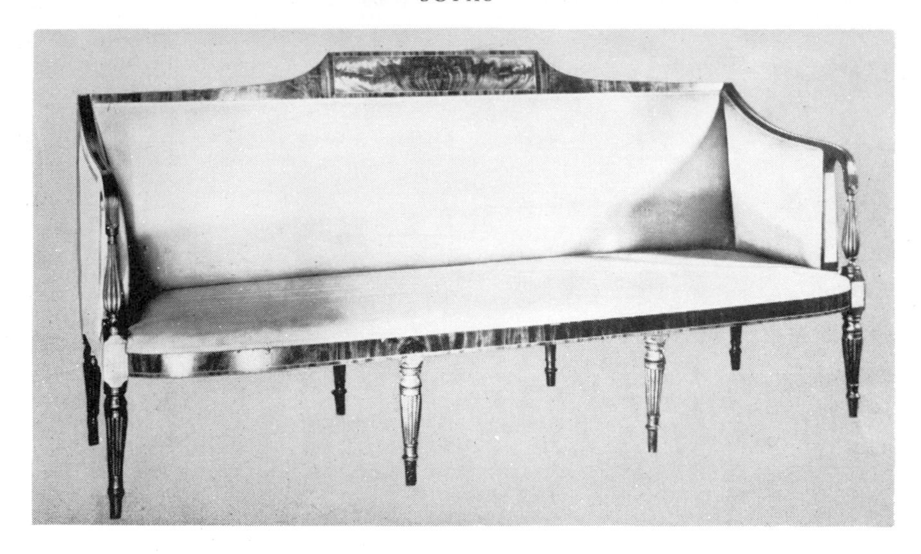

BETTER

Sheraton mahogany sofa with center panel in back, Salem, Massachusetts, circa 1800. A Salem sofa of fine line and quality.

BEST

Sheraton mahogany sofa, carved by Samuel McIntire, Salem, Mass., circa 1800. An American classic. This sofa was probably made by a fine Salem craftsman and then carved to order by Samuel McIntire. The basket of fruit was a favorite motif of McIntire's and is found in some of the finest Salem furniture and architecture of the late eighteenth century.

GOOD

Sheraton mahogany small sofa, New England, circa 1800. A crude angular sofa which even a fine upholstery job could not make desirable.

BEST

Sheraton mahogany small sofa, Salem, Mass., circa 1800. This and the sofa illustrated above are shown together because both exhibit the exposed mahogany arm rests extending up to the back. That feature plus the fact they were both made during the same era are their only similarities. The contrast in quality and line is far more striking than the similarity of type.

GOOD

Sheraton mahogony sofa with three-panel carved back, New York, circa 1800. A clumsy sofa with heavy roll arms and stumpy reeded legs.

BEST

Sheraton mahogany sofa with three-panel carved back, by Duncan Phyfe, New York, circa 1800. This outstanding Phyfe sofa was made for Rufus King, famous New York statesman and Ambassador to England. It was purchased from a direct descendant and is now in a private collection. It was the most expensive type that Phyfe produced and remains so today.

GOOD

Sheraton mahogany sofa, New York, circa 1800. A thoroughly undesirable specimen of angular line and a broad veneered crest which does not blend with the rest of the piece. The humped arms were never as successful as the conventional reeded Phyfe arm shown in the sofa illustrated below.

BEST

Sheraton mahogany sofa with three-panel carved back, by Duncan Phyfe, New York, circa 1800. Cornucopia center and sheaf of wheat on end panels. Known as the Danielson sofa. A fine Phyfe sofa with an excellent carved back and an interesting spiral molding above the reeded legs. Now in a private collection.

GOOD

Left. Windsor settee, American, circa 1800. A primitive example of little merit. It gives the effect of a group of unrelated parts carelessly stuck together with no unity of purpose.

BETTER

Below. Windsor settee, American, circa 1780. A better example, in which all parts are integrated. The serpentine arms flow nicely into the back and the seat is well shaped. The bamboo turnings are weak compared to those of the example illustrated at bottom of page.

BEST

Windsor settee, New England, circa 1770. A choice example of beautiful form and most desirable turnings. Note the effective rake to the legs and arm supports.

GOOD

Early tavern table, Pennsylvania, circa 1680-1710. Pleasing tavern table, but with mediocre turnings.

BETTER

Early tavern table, Pennsylvania, circa 1680-1710. Tavern table with better than average turnings.

BEST

Pilgrim tavern table, New England, circa 1680-1710. Superb tavern table with the finest turnings. Note the finial in the center of the scalloped apron.

BEST

Pilgrim tuckaway table, New England, circa 1680-1710. One can only speak of this rare American innovation in superlatives, from the standpoint of ingenuity, beauty and functionalism. Note the butterfly wings, more commonly found in "butterfly" tables.

BEST

Oval-top tavern table with triangular scalloped frame, New England, circa 1680-1710. Choice tavern table. A rare and most desirable type. One of the very few tavern tables made with a triangular base and with a graceful scalloped apron.

BEST

Oval-top tavern table, New England, circa 1680-1710. The vase and ring turnings are superlative. Note the natural wear on the stretchers.

GOOD

Pilgrim joint stool, New England, circa 1680-1720. A crude early specimen which lacks the refinement of the two tables illustrated below and the one at right; it is, therefore, much less valuable even though the type is exceedingly rare. The thick top has no molded edge; the table lacks an apron or frame, so that the top appears disjointed. The turnings are relatively primitive.

BEST

Pilgrim joint stool, Rhode Island, circa 1680-1720. A prize specimen, with a fine quarter round molding to the top and the best turnings.

BETTER

Pilgrim joint stool, Rhode Island, circa 1680-1720. A fine quality example which has suffered the damage common to this period—the rotting and loss of the turned feet. The vase and ring turnings are fine, and the lower edge of the top is beveled to relieve the thick appearance so apparent in the example shown directly above.

BEST

Pilgrim joint stool, New England, circa 1680-1720. One of the finest joint stools known, with the almost unique feature of a drawer in one end.

The Pilgrim butterfly table, so called because of its shaped wings, is a delightful and popular American creation. Because of the rarity and value of genuine examples, they have been faked more often than any other type of early table. These fakes run the gamut from obvious frauds to clever adaptations, employing the base of an old tavern table and the top of an old drop leaf table.

GOOD

Pilgrim butterfly table, New England, circa 1680-1710. Probably a unique variety of the butterfly table, but less valuable than the other examples shown on this page because it is of lesser quality. The legs have no splay and also lack turnings of any quality.

BETTER

Pilgrim butterfly table, New England, circa 1680-1710. A desirable table with average turnings and finely shaped butterfly wings.

BETTER

Pilgrim butterfly table, New England, circa 1680-1710. An attractive small example with a fine splay to the legs and average turnings. The butterfly wings are shapeless and detract from the beauty of the table.

BEST

Pilgrim butterfly table, New England, circa 1680-1710. Superlative table of small size, ripe turnings and finely shaped wings. Compact and with a bold splay to the legs, such a table alone could make any collection notable.

BEST

Pilgrim gateleg table, New England, circa 1680-1710. Choice large-size gateleg table with excellent turnings. These tables were used extensively throughout the Colonies and remained the most popular type of dining table from 1680 to 1720 in New England, Pennsylvania and Virginia. The examples such as this one, which have survived intact, are highly prized. Many have had the feet rotted away because of dampness and the tops were abused and replaced.

BEST

Right. Gateleg table, Pennsylvania, circa 1680-1710. An outstanding table, with bold vase and ring turnings.

BEST

Below. Pilgrim gateleg table, Rhode Island, circa 1680-1710. A Rhode Island table which is the envy of any collector of Pilgrim furniture. The turnings are perfect and the trumpet feet are possibly unique.

Close-up view of turnings of table directly at left.

GOOD

A primitive chair table or hutch table, New England, circa 1680. These early examples of functional design served two purposes in the Pilgrim all-purpose kitchen. In the view shown, one could sit in front of the fire, and the solid back would protect against drafts. When the hinged top was lowered, it formed a table. This example shows that no effort was made to create a beautiful as well as a useful article.

BEST

A Pilgrim hutch table of great distinction, New England, circa 1680. Created under the same adverse conditions as the table shown above. How can we excuse the crudity of the other table if this craftsman, working in the same locality at the same time, made this example beautiful as well as useful. Note the clever employment of a drawer under the seat.

GOOD

Queen Anne walnut drop-leaf dining table, Philadelphia, circa 1720-1750. Crude cousin to the table shown below. Exaggerated curve to leg makes it look weak at ankles like a novice ice skater. The drake feet were formed by mere incisions.

BEST

Queen Anne walnut dining table, Philadelphia, circa 1720-1750. A remarkable comparison with the example shown above of a superficially similar table, but made by a talented artisan. Note the balanced curve to the cabriole leg, which is in perfect proportion, also the more careful and effective treatment of the drake foot.

GOOD

Left. Chippendale claw and ball foot walnut dining table, American, circa 1750-1780. Some ungifted carpenter saw a table like the one shown at left below and decided to try his hand at it, with unfortunate results. Obviously the apron is too deep, the leg is crudely formed and the claw and ball foot is patterned on a very sick bird.

Right. A study in crudity—detail of table shown to the left. In evolution this would be considered an embryo and would be an early stage of development. But this table was made during the same era and possibly later than the example shown at left below. Many crude items are excused because they are called "early." The excuse is seldom a valid one.

BETTER

Chippendale claw and ball foot walnut dining table, American, circa 1750-1780. This is the most sharply pointed-up contrast in the book, for the type is identical with that of the table shown at left above, but the results are poles apart.

BEST

Chippendale mahogany dining table, Rhode Island, circa 1750-1780. A magnificent table of the close-grained San Dominican mahogany used extensively by the great Newport craftsmen. The table exhibits perfect symmetry enhanced by the oval-shaped top. The cabriole legs have a bold successful curve and superbly modeled claw and ball feet. The scalloped apron is more beautifully executed than that on either of the two other examples shown on this page.

GOOD

Hepplewhite mahogany inlaid dining table, Maryland, circa 1780. The placement of the inlay is not well planned and therefore loses most of its effect. The line inlay on the legs would have been considerably more effective if it had terminated in an inlaid band, as on the table illustrated below.

BEST

Hepplewhite mahogany inlaid dining table, Maryland, circa 1780. An outstanding table, distinguished by the superb bellflower inlay on the slender tapered legs. The rectangular line inlay on the apron more effectively relieves this expanse than does the oval inlay on the table shown above, because it conforms to the shape of the panel.

Three extension mahogany dining tables made in New York between 1800-1820. All three tables can be extended to form large banquet tables by an ingenious accordion or slide device which when extended holds a number of extra leaves. All three tables were made by Duncan Phyfe, or one of his contemporaries, in New York City, and all the large single-piece tops are made of select, naturally dried solid mahogany which is hardly obtainable today. Because these tops were fully dried before the tables were constructed, they never warped or changed shape through these many years.

GOOD

This, the poorest of the three, was made by a great craftsman who unfortunately catered to the degenerating tastes of the Empire period. The massiveness of the pedestal is not necessary for proper support of the table and the deep apron helps to make this a clumsy specimen.

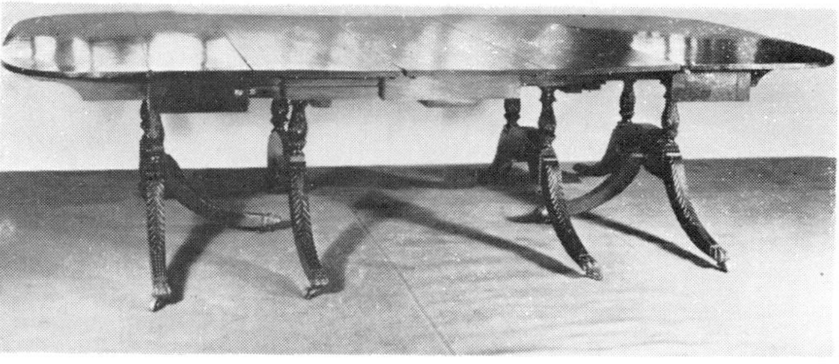

Side view of table illustrated directly below, partially extended and with a glimpse of the slide framework. The functional ingenuity of this table belies the modernists who claim that functionalism was invented in the twentieth century. This table was so well preserved by the several generations of succeeding owners that it retained its original pine-slotted storage box made to hold the extra mahogany leaves.

BEST

End view of fine Phyfe table with two slender turned columns supporting each section.

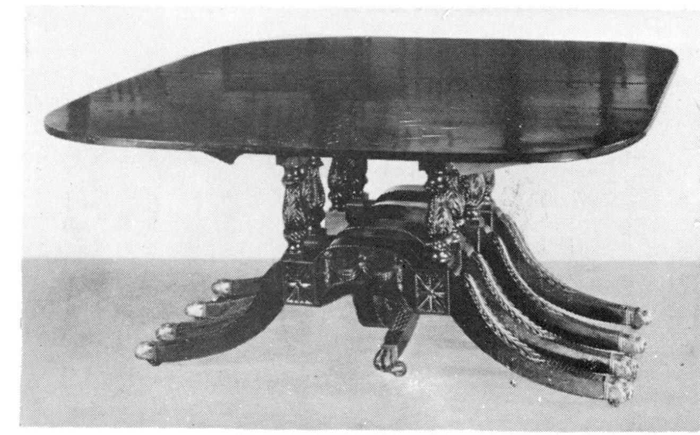

BEST

End view of a great masterpiece by Duncan Phyfe and one of his crowning achievements. When the drop leaves at each end are closed, the table reduces to a length of twenty-five inches—when fully extended it measures thirteen feet. To the best of our knowledge, the acanthus leaf carving on the legs and columns occurs in no other extension table by Duncan Phyfe.

BETTER

Queen Anne small-size drop-leaf or tea table with square leaves, New England, circa 1720-1750. The cabriole legs have a rather stiff, straight feeling. Nevertheless, it is a desirable table.

BEST

Queen Anne small-size drop-leaf table, New England, circa 1720-1750. A collector's dream realized—a superb example of this extremely rare type. Few of these tiny tables were made, and this one has the additional attraction of undisputed descent in the family of John Hancock. This association enhances a fine table but would have little effect on a mediocre or poor example.

BEST

One of two or three New England Queen Anne "tuckaway" tables, circa 1720-1750. Certainly a priceless example of the ingenuity of Colonial craftsmen. When closed, the legs swing together, the top folds to a vertical position and table can be tucked into a closet.

BEST

Queen Anne porringer-top tea table, Rhode Island, circa 1720-1750. These desirable, well-executed tables are known to have been made in Newport and Providence, but some may have been fashioned in other parts of New England. The shaped corners seem adapted to hold the silver or pewter porringers of that era.

BEST

Rare cherry tray-top tea table, Connecticut, circa 1720-1750. Note the graceful cabriole leg and scalloped apron. This table admirably expresses the charm and individuality of our Connecticut craftsmen.

BEST

Queen Anne walnut tea table with drawer, New England, circa 1720-1750. A true American classic. Observe the symmetry of the table as a whole and the brilliant touches of a gifted artisan. His successful introduction of the drawer in one end and the notched corners of the tray molding make this table one of the great rarities of its type. It would still be a priceless table without these innovations.

BEST

The supreme American Chippendale tea table, made by John Goddard of Newport, R. I., circa 1750-1780. This masterpiece of design as well as execution is enough proof by itself of the creative genius of our American craftsmen. There is no form even remotely resembling it in England or the Continent. Is it any wonder that lovers of Americana get angry when they hear that our Colonial cabinetmakers merely copied the English. Note the open claw and ball foot which is found only in Newport pieces.

GOOD

Left. Chippendale mahogany Pembroke table with arched stretchers supporting an unusual platform, Philadelphia, circa 1750-1780. A rare type but fairly provincial in execution. The square drop leaves with the deep overhang lend a boxy appearance to the table and the stretchers are not expertly shaped.

BEST

Below. Chippendale mahogany Pembroke table with arched stretchers, Philadelphia, circa 1750-1780. A choice and rare table. A completely successful interpretation of an original design. Note how the shaped leaves complement the beautifully arched stretchers which proudly terminate in the effective turned finial.

BETTER

Left. Chippendale mahogany Pembroke table with finely arched stretchers, Philadelphia, circa 1750-1780. A good quality Pembroke table. The only criticism is the evidence in the illustration below of what a master craftsman achieved from the same model by shaping the leaves and adding spiral and gadroon moldings as well as the blocked feet.

BEST

Below. Chippendale mahogany Pembroke table with finely arched stretchers, Philadelphia, circa 1750-1780. Note the strength imparted to this masterpiece by the blocked "Marlborough" feet and the grace added by the beautifully shaped leaves with the molded edges. In many cases overambitious craftsmen added details which were superfluous and would have been better eliminated. In the hands of this brilliant artisan, however, the spiral beading in the legs and the carved gadroon molding of the apron blend in with the design, and one would hate to see them eliminated. Any collector would get a bargain if he obtained this table at ten times the value of the one shown above.

All three mahogany tables illustrated on this page were made in the vicinity of Boston shortly after the Revolution and are excellent examples of a close association in type and a wide divergence in quality.

GOOD

Hepplewhite mahogany Pembroke table with serpentine leaves, New England, circa 1760-1780. The long deep leaves seem to overpower the rest of the table.

BETTER

Hepplewhite mahogany Pembroke table with serpentine leaves, New England, circa 1760-1780. The molded legs and crossed stretchers add refinement and balance. The shallow leaves are not in perfect ratio to the size of the table.

BEST

Hepplewhite mahogany Pembroke table with serpentine leaves, New England, circa 1760-1780. A brilliant and skillful rendition: the pierced stretchers are beautifully done as are the pierced corner brackets, hardly visible in this photograph. A choice collector's table.

While the form of the Hepplewhite Pembroke table originated in England, the original and beautiful treatments of the better New York and Baltimore examples have made them justly famous in their own right. A few superlative tables of this type were made also in Newport, New England, New Jersey and Philadelphia.

GOOD

Hepplewhite cherry inlaid Pembroke table, New York, circa 1780. A mediocre table with thick top and uninteresting plain apron.

BEST

Hepplewhite mahogany inlaid Pembroke table, New York, circa 1780. A Pembroke table of restrained inlay but fine quality. This table is far more desirable than a more elaborate example of lesser quality.

BEST

Hepplewhite mahogany inlaid Pembroke table, New York, circa 1780. A table with inverted cup inlay and the book inlay above. Most of the fine tables of this period have the oval-shaped tops and the same careful attention to detail such as the cross-banding at the lower portion of the legs and the line inlay bordering the edges of the drawer and top.

BEST

Hepplewhite mahogany Pembroke table with bellflower inlay, Baltimore, circa 1780. The acme of perfection of design in a bellflower inlaid table. Note the oval inlaid panel breaking the monotony of the drawer front. This table nobly passes the test of any inlaid table—does any of the inlay seem superfluous?

GOOD

Left. Hepplewhite mahogany inlaid Pembroke table, Baltimore, circa 1780. A startling comparison between two Baltimore inlaid tables is shown on this page. Not only is the inlay of this table crowded and overdone, but the thick square leaves give a heavy appearance to the top. This example is proof of the fact that detail alone, such as inlay or carving, no matter how rare or abundant, does not create value unless it is expertly placed and successfully used.

BEST

Below. Hepplewhite mahogany inlaid Pembroke table, Baltimore, circa 1780. A masterpiece of American design and craftsmanship. Note the horizontal cross-banding on the legs, which serves as a background for the choice typical Baltimore bellflower.

GOOD

Left. Sheraton mahogany Pembroke table with clover leaves, New York, circa 1800. A poor specimen with heavy spiral legs. The table is too long for the proper relation to the width, and the clover leaf is poorly shaped.

BEST

Below. Sheraton mahogany Pembroke table with serpentine leaves, New York, circa 1800. A delicate harmonious example with slender reeded legs, by Duncan Phyfe. The leaves are of particularly beautiful shape, and are in perfect balance. This reeded leg, with the bulbous foot, offers strong evidence of Duncan Phyfe's handiwork. It was made in various degrees of thickness; this slender leg is associated with Phyfe's earlier and more desirable period.

BETTER

Sheraton mahogany library table with acanthus carving on legs, New York, circa 1800-1815. The pedestal is heavy and the legs do not have enough spread to counter-balance the top.

BEST

Sheraton mahogany library table with acanthus carving on the legs, by Duncan Phyfe, New York, circa 1800-1815. Note how the additional splay of the legs of this fine Phyfe table gives it better balance. The superb urn pedestal is in startling contrast to that of the table shown above.

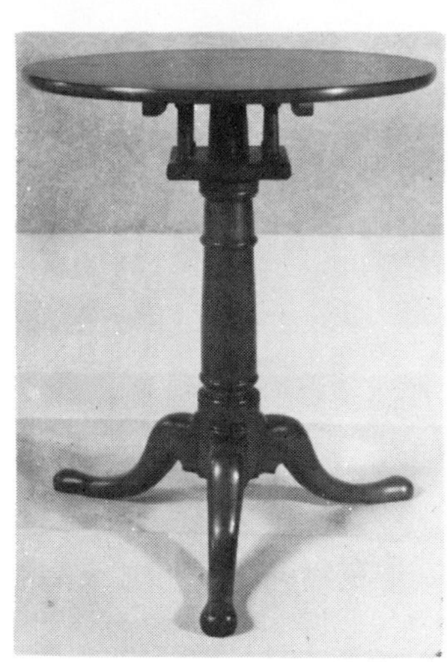

GOOD

Chippendale mahogany tripod tip and turn table, Philadelphia, circa 1750-1780. A poor specimen with shapeless pedestal, abbreviated knees and sagging ankles.

BETTER

Chippendale mahogany tripod tip and turn table, Philadelphia, circa 1750-1780. An average example with a thick bulbous pedestal.

BEST

Chippendale mahogany tripod tip and turn table, Philadelphia, circa 1750-1780. A perfectly proportioned table. Note the fully developed pad feet, the highly desired ball and ring turning and slender shaft, the bulbous-shaped birdcage support and the raised dish rim, all features demanded in a high-priced example.

GOOD

Chippendale mahogany tip and turn table with birdcage support, Philadelphia, circa 1750-1780. The urn-shaped pedestal is too big and heavy for this small table and the legs are a little stumpy.

BEST

Chippendale mahogany tip and turn table with birdcage supports, Philadelphia, circa 1750-1780. The urn is in proper relation to the pedestal and the legs are well shaped. A fine example.

BEST

Chippendale mahogany tripod tip table with serpentine top, Boston, circa 1750-1780. A choice tip table. It affords an excellent view of the superbly figured solid mahogany. A well-balanced table of fine quality. The fine molded edge of the top eliminates any objectionable appearance of thickness. The cabriole legs are well formed and terminate in fine pad feet with platforms.

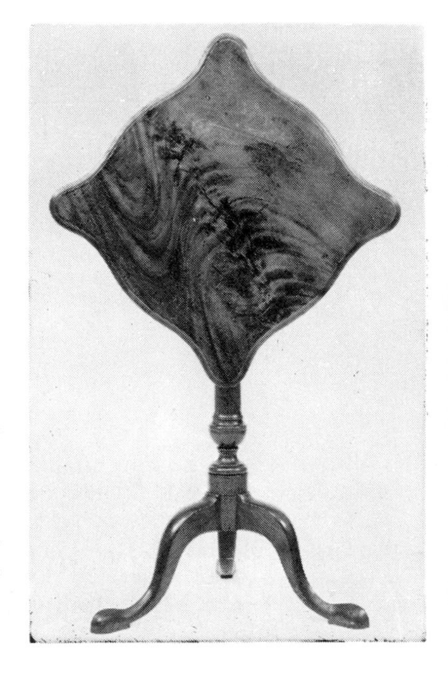

GOOD

Chippendale tripod table, Pennsylvania, circa 1750-1780. Clumsy tripod table with heavy pedestal and crudely shaped legs. Notice that the thigh of this table, as in many primitive examples, has straight sides and is the same thickness from top to bottom, whereas the more accomplished examples, such as the one shown below, are thicker and more rounded at the thigh and more slender at the ankle.

BEST

Chippendale cherry tripod table, Philadelphia, circa 1750-1780. A superbly proportioned cherry tripod table with finely modeled legs and well-shaped pedestal. Note the finely shaped pad feet compared with the shapeless feet of the table shown above, also the bold lift to the ankle on this Philadelphia pre-Revolutionary table.

BETTER

Chippendale mahogany tripod table, Philadelphia, circa 1750-1780. A relatively clumsy pedestal, especially when compared with the example illustrated below.

BEST

Chippendale mahogany tripod table, Philadelphia, circa 1750-1780. This highly prized example has an exceptionally well-turned pedestal and a very fine cabriole leg. Note the lift to the ankles.

BETTER

Tip and turn table with carved knees and claw and ball feet, Philadelphia, circa 1750-1780. A good table and a scarce type. But the pedestal is somewhat heavy, the legs are too spindly at the thighs and the claw and ball feet are not as bold or as crisp as those of the table shown below.

BEST

One of the supreme Philadelphia tip and turn tables, circa 1750-1780. The base is a model of perfection, and it is crowned by a piecrust top; one of the few such tables in this small size to have survived.

BEST

View of the center table with the top tipped to its vertical position. Remember that this top, with its finely scalloped edge, is carved from a solid piece of mahogany.

GOOD

Chippendale tripod tip and turn table, Philadelphia, circa 1770. A poor example, with spiderlike legs, primitive claw and ball feet and shapeless pedestal.

BETTER

Chippendale tripod tip and turn table, Philadelphia, circa 1770. A finer example than the table shown at left, with raised dish rim and better cabriole leg—but the pedestal is clumsy.

BEST

Chippendale tripod tip and turn table, Philadelphia, circa 1770. The outstanding proportions, finely turned pedestal and crisp claw and ball feet make this a very desirable table.

GOOD

Chippendale large tripod tip and turn table, Philadelphia, circa 1750-1780. A view of a grossly inferior table with the top tilted

BEST

Chippendale large tripod tip and turn table, Philadelphia, circa 1750-1780. View of a fine table, with top tilted, with the best cabriole legs, crisp claw and ball feet and raised dish rim which is carved from tne solid rather than applied. The top is in proper ratio to the base and does not overwhelm it as is so clearly demonstrated in the example shown above.

GOOD

Chippendale mahogany piecrust table, Philadelphia, circa 1750-1780. An uninspired specimen with embryo claw and ball feet and uninteresting thick pedestal.

BETTER

Chippendale mahogany piecrust table with carved knees and turned pedestal, Philadelphia, circa 1750-1780. An unsuccessful base with a heavy pedestal and abbreviated cabriole legs ending in weak claw and ball feet.

BEST

Chippendale mahogany piecrust table with carved knees and turned pedestal, Philadelphia, circa 1750-1780. One of the great piecrust tables, whose high standing lies in its superlative proportions. To some lovers of Americana it expresses in its simplicity and dignity one of the greatest contributions of our eighteenth century culture. Now in a private collection.

BETTER

Chippendale piecrust table, Philadelphia, circa 1750-1780. This example has a unique feature of gadrooning at the base, but the pedestal is somewhat crude and the leg is not the best form. The thigh isn't rounded and the knee seems to project too far for proper symmetry.

BEST

Chippendale piecrust table, Philadelphia, circa 1750-1780. A superlative table with a highly successful and balanced pedestal of unusual form.

GOOD

Left. Chippendale large tripod tip and turn table with carved knees, Pennsylvania, circa 1750-1780. An anemic-looking specimen with a crudely formed pedestal and a weak cabriole leg and claw and ball foot. Not worth one tenth the value of the example shown below.

BEST

Below. Chippendale large tripod tip and turn table with carved knees, Pennsylvania, circa 1750-1780. A masterpiece, and important for its vigorous beauty. Note the bold stance to the cabriole legs and the crisp knuckles on the claw and ball feet. This table would be fine without carving; the fine, deep, well-placed carving places it in the highest category. Courtesy of Museum of Fine Arts, Boston, M. & M. Karolik Collection.

GOOD

Left. Hepplewhite mahogany candlestand with urn pedestal, New England, circa 1780. A crude version of little merit. The pedestal is too fat above the urn. The legs show no refinemen and do not reduce in thickness at the ankle as do the legs of every tripod table produced by a fine artisan.

BEST

Below. Hepplewhite mahogany candlestands with urn pedestals, New England, circa 1780. A pair of choice candlestands, rarely found in pairs. Compare the slenderness of the column with the heaviness of the example shown above. Also compare the subtly shaped leg ending in a spade foot with the crude stumps in the other table.

GOOD

Left. Late Sheraton mahogany sewing table, New York, circa 1820. An abuse of our national bird, this monstrosity is proof of the old adage "Fine feathers do not make a fine bird." It proves the fundamental principle of logic that no matter how much you build on a false premise, the result is wrong. No matter how much or how excellent the carving, placed on a piece of poor form, the result is a failure.

BETTER

Right. Sheraton mahogany octagonal sewing table, New York, circa 1800-1815. A good table, with too much pedestal and too little body.

BETTER

Sheraton mahogany octagonal sewing table, New York, circa 1800-1815. Similar to one at right, attributed to Phyfe but far less desirable. It exhibits a clumsy pedestal and cramped legs. While this table has as much, or more, work in its construction, and as finely figured veneer as has the table to the right, it would not be considered at any price by most collectors who would pay a premium for its superior.

BEST

Sheraton mahogany octagonal sewing table, New York, circa 1800-1815. A masterpiece by Duncan Phyfe at his best period, this table exhibits the perfection of balance and proportion of which Phyfe was capable when he was not catering to the degenerating tastes of the Empire influence. The tambour front opens to exhibit an intricate and useful arrangement of compartments. Now in a private collection.

GOOD

Sheraton mahogany sewing table, New York, circa 1800-1810. A heavy table of little merit. The spiral legs are seldom if ever successful.

BETTER

Sheraton mahogany sewing table, New York, circa 1800-1810. A table whose form is similar to that of the table shown at bottom of page, but of considerably poorer quality. Compare the center sections between the reeded columns.

BEST

Sheraton mahogany sewing table, New York, circa 1800-1810. A fine, well-proportioned table of excellent quality and beautifully figured veneers. Incidentally, the veneers used in the eighteenth century pieces are fifty to one hundred times as thick as modern veneers, which is primarily the reason that they have remained intact on so many antique pieces.

GOOD

Sheraton mahogany "bandbox" sewing table, New York, circa 1800-1810. A mediocre table which has a long way to go to reach the exalted heights of the table illustrated at right below.

BEST

Sheraton mahogany tambour sewing table, New York, circa 1800-1815. A masterpiece by Duncan Phyfe, now in the Edison Institute, Dearbon, Michigan.

BEST

Sheraton mahogany tambour sewing table, New York, circa 1800-1810. A masterpiece by Duncan Phyfe, with beautiful, slender, reeded legs. Note the designs created by the carefully matched veneers, a favorite device of Phyfe. This open view shows the variety of uses to which this compact table can be put. Now in the Edison Institute, Dearborn, Michigan.

BEST

Sheraton mahogany "bandbox" sewing table, New York, circa 1800-1810. A masterpiece by Duncan Phyfe, with his typical reeded leg and bulbous foot. Note the quality and fine subdued detail in the body.

GOOD

Hepplewhite cherry inlaid bedside table with shaped top, New England, circa 1780-1800. An unsuccessful attempt at a difficult design. The top and the base look somewhat disjointed, probably caused by having too little overhang at the front and too much at the side. The crude legs do not have enough taper.

BEST

Hepplewhite curly maple inlaid bedside table with shaped top, New England, circa 1780-1800. A successful achievement of a difficult design. The beautifully shaped top blends harmoniously with the base. The legs are finely tapered and the beaded edges of the legs and the diagonal border of inlay below the drawer are effective touches.

GOOD

Sheraton bedside table, Salem, Mass., circa 1800. A terrific letdown after looking at the table at right below. One might say, "I like this table better because I love simplicity." Well, strip the Seymour table of all its veneer and its reeding—it is still vastly superior in form to this table. Simplicity with dignity, yes — simplicity with crudity, vastly overrated.

GOOD

Sheraton mahogany bedside table, Boston, Mass., circa 1800. A mediocre table of the same general form as the masterpiece shown at right below, but possessing little merit. The coarse reeding begins and ends nowhere, and the spool turning is heavy and coarse.

View of top of Seymour table. Obviously a labor of love, the magnificently figured veneer of exotic wood is framed within borders of curly maple and mahogany. Probably a unique interpretation.

BEST

Sheraton mahogany bedside table, Boston, circa 1800. This superlative table was fashioned by one of the greatest and deservedly famous Boston craftsman, John Seymour. The half-ring inlaid border of the top was a favorite pattern of this maker. Note how the figured curly maple and satinwood is all contained within banded borders and not splashed over a large surface on the front or sides. This allows the table to have so much detail and yet not appear flamboyant. Note the height and grace of the legs which this expert craftsman, with an eye sensitive to proportion, felt were necessary to compensate for the width of the body. Note how the fine tapered reeding is contained in a turning at both ends, as it should be in any desirable table.

GOOD

Sheraton bedside table, American, circa 1800. A boxy table with crudely turned legs. It has too much leg and too little body.

BEST

Sheraton sewing table, Salem, Mass., circa 1800. A Sheraton octagonal top sewing table of fine quality. Note the curly mahogany drawer fronts. The octagonal-shaped top relieves any feeling of boxiness. The slender legs are well turned and finely reeded.

BEST

Sheraton mahogany sewing table, Salem, Mass., circa 1800. This exceptional table has an ingenious double ratchet arrangement which allows the top to lift to this position, revealing several covered compartments which were meant to contain sewing implements. When the top is lowered, this arrangement is not suspected. Note the finely carved edge of the top, typical of the work of William Hook, one of the greatest Salem craftsmen. The pull-out slide at the side originally held a bag compartment.

GOOD

Sheraton mahogany sewing table with bag, New England, circa 1800. This hopelessly crude table cannot properly be called an antique. Webster defines an antique as "an object of ancient art." This table is ancient but not art. It and examples of similar quality are wrongly treasured by those who think that our early culture was primitive. That this is not so is proved by the table illustrated below, which fulfills the same purpose but is a work of art. It is not the simplicity of this table that is criticized—it is the ineptness of the craftsmanship, the turnings and the thick, heavy top.

BEST

Sheraton mahogany and satinwood sewing table with bag, Salem, Mass., circa 1800. This exquisite American classic is one of a number of superb sewing tables created by Salem craftsmen. The flame satinwood, the restrained inlaid borders are all carefully matched and blended. The reeded legs are delicate but not spindly and the proportions are unsurpassed.

GOOD

Above. Sheraton bedside table, American, circa 1800. A crude boxy table with clumsy turned legs.

BETTER

Above. Sheraton bedside table with scalloped shelf, Salem, Mass., circa 1800. An example of lesser quality than the table shown left below. It is not as delicate and the scalloping is cruder.

BEST

Left. Sheraton bedside table with scalloped shelf, Salem, Mass., circa 1800. This very scarce type of mahogany and satinwood table is highly prized by collectors—in this quality. Note that the flame satinwood is contained within cross-banded borders and inlaid borders on the stiles. This refinement is consistently present in the fine Salem mahogany and satinwood tables of the period, and succeeds in avoiding flamboyancy.

GOOD

Queen Anne mahogany console table with marble top, New Jersey or Pennsylvania, circa 1740-1760. An undistinguished table with a thick marble top, unrelieved by a molded edge, such as the two other tables illustrated here have. The leg descends practically in a vertical line from the knee and does not have the serpentine curve required in a fine cabriole leg. The feet are underdeveloped and the plain straight apron is monotonous.

BEST

Chippendale mahogany console table with marble top, New England, circa 1750-1770. An outstanding table with a fine scalloped apron and molded top which relieves any appearance of thickness. The cabriole leg is well formed as is the claw and ball foot.

BEST

Chippendale mahogany console table with marble top, Philadelphia, circa 1750-1780. A great masterpiece of design and execution. The front is brilliantly shaped and the apron is effectively relieved by the bold gadroon molding. The curve of the cabriole leg and the modeling of the claw and ball foot are perfection itself, as is the carving on the knee. Certainly one of the greatest, if not the greatest, console tables produced in the Colonies. Courtesy of the Museum of Fine Arts, Boston, M. & M. Karolik Collection.

GOOD

Above. Sheraton mahogany serving table, Salem, Mass., circa 1800. A good table which, however, seems to have too much body for its short legs.

BEST

Above. Sheraton mahogany and maple dressing table, Salem, Mass., circa 1800. One of several fine pieces of this type produced by Salem craftsmen, it served a useful function as well as being a thing of beauty. The successful blending of the scrolled mirror supports with the rest of the body of the piece is worthy of admiration. Note the fine cross-banded borders of the drawers.

BEST

Sheraton mahogany and satinwood serving table, Salem, Mass., circa 1800. A very choice example of a scarce type. The proportions leave nothing to be desired and the sides as well as the front are serpentine.

GOOD

Sheraton mahogany serving table, Salem, Mass., circa 1800. An inferior table, with little to recommend it either in design or workmanship. The reeded legs do not have sufficient height in relation to the wide frame. The concave curve in the frame breaks too suddenly.

BETTER

Sheraton mahogany serving table, Salem, Mass., circa 1800. An amazing comparison with the example illustrated at left below because undoubtedly both tables were made in the same shop, yet this table exhibits poor proportions in that the legs are too short and chunky. Also surprising is the fact that the carving is relatively heavy and coarse—apparently not the hand of the master carver of Salem. Is it possible that William Hook had a customer who did not want to pay the higher price, and therefore Hook did the carving himself—with indifferent success?

BEST

Sheraton mahogany serving table, Salem, Mass., circa 1800. A choice table of fine proportions and excellent details. The distinctive border of the top shows evidence of the work of William Hook, who probably made the table and gave it to McIntire to be carved. This specialization was a frequent practice, and in this case the cabinetmaker and the carver blended a masterpiece.

BETTER

Chippendale mahogany card table, Philadelphia, circa 1750-1780. A card table of above-average quality. The cabriole legs and claw and ball feet are well formed. The unfinished appearance of the apron indicates why a superior craftsman, such as the one who fashioned the table at the right, added a gadroon molding. The drawer of this table would be more effective if it were smaller.

BEST

Chippendale mahogany card table, Philadelphia, circa 1750-1780. A choice table with an excellent leg and finely carved knee. The gadroon molding is most effective.

BEST

Chippendale mahogany card table, Philadelphia, circa 1750-1780. A magnificent table with shaped corners, the finest carved knees and beautifully scalloped apron. A priceless example of Philadelphia genius.

BEST

Chippendale mahogany card table, Salem, Mass., circa 1750-1780. One of the most graceful American card tables, with a beautifully scalloped apron and finely carved knees with the punchwork background frequently employed by the Salem carvers.

BEST

Chippendale mahogany card table, by John Goddard, Newport, R. I., circa 1750-1780. This masterpiece by the Dean of New England craftsmen shows great originality of contour and boldness of line. It exhibits typical Goddard carving and open claw and ball feet.

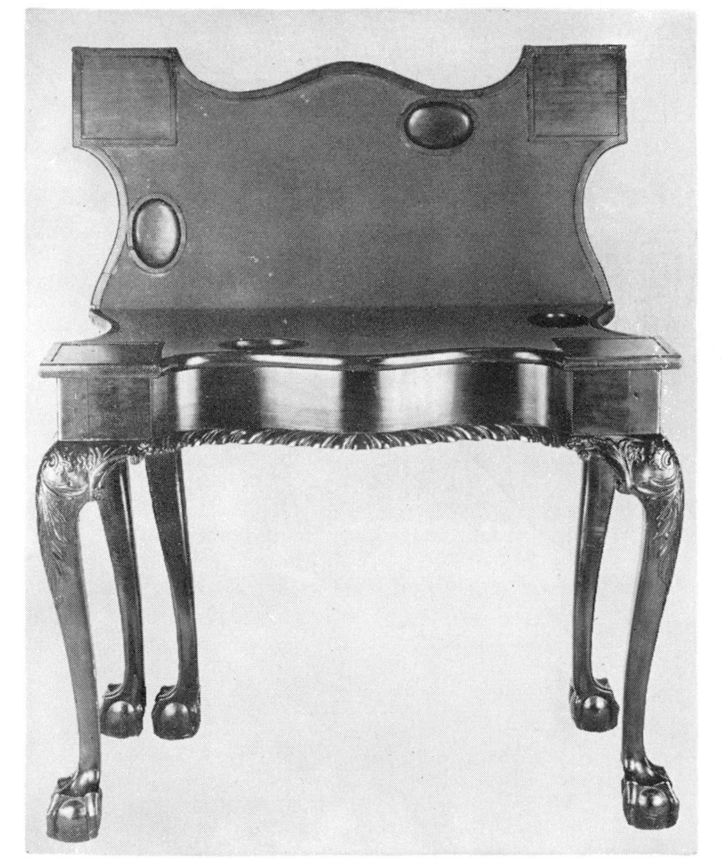

BEST

Chippendale mahogany serpentine-front card table, New York, circa 1750-1780. A superlative five-legged card table with typical New York carving on the knees and the familiar gadroon molding. Note the desirable pockets in the top.

BETTER

Chippendale mahogany card table, Philadelphia, circa 1750-1780. A good table with pierced corner brackets, which do not completely relieve the boxy tendency inherent in this style of table.

BEST

Chippendale mahogany card table, Philadelphia, circa 1750-1780. A masterpiece of Philadelphia craftsmanship, this table shows the grandeur the artisan was able to obtain from a simple form The serpentine-shaped front and sides, the fluted legs and vigorous blocked feet make this table a prize for any collector. Courtesy of Museum of Fine Arts, Boston, M. & M. Karolik Collection.

GOOD

Hepplewhite mahogany card table, Newport, R. I., circa 1780. A crude table by an ungifted craftsman who used the table shown at right for a model. He neglected to shape the body or the apron, making the shaped top appear disjointed.

BETTER

Hepplewhite mahogany card table, Newport, R. I., circa 1780. A mediocre table derived from the same inspiration but lacking the imagination of the example shown below. The legs are heavy and not stop-fluted and the apron is not shaped.

BEST

Hepplewhite mahogany card table, Newport, R. I., circa 1780. This diminutive masterpiece is sufficiently like a labeled example in the Metropolitan Museum to identify it as the work of John Townsend. The blocked serpentine front and shaped apron with notched carving make a brilliant design. The effective stop-fluting on the legs was a favored device of John Townsend.

Side view of Townsend table, showing the beautifully shaped side and the bold contour of the front.

GOOD

Hepplewhite mahogany inlaid card table, New England, circa 1780-1800. A mediocre table. The bulge in the center apron does not form one convex curve from leg to leg, as in the better tables, but begins straight and suddenly protrudes. The oval in the center of the apron has no border and the bandings of inlay are relatively inept. This is a five-legged card table, considered rare, but this example is considerably less valuable than the one shown to the right, and worth only a small fraction of its value.

BEST

Hepplewhite mahogany inlaid card table, New England, circa 1780-1800. A choice table of restrained beauty and fine balance. Note the finely banded borders of inlay. The additional taper of the legs below the inlaid cuffs is a feature found only in a few choice Salem and Boston tables.

BEST

Hepplewhite mahogany and satinwood card table, Salem, Mass., circa 1780-1800. A masterpiece of design and detail. We consider this to be the finest Hepplewhite card table produced in New England. Note how the line inlay on the legs contains horizontal cross-banding. The division of the center apron into three sections is very effective and the rectangular panels above the legs are a delightful touch by this brilliant artisan. Note the narrowness of the apron in relation to the height of the legs, achieving great delicacy.

BEST

Hepplewhite mahogany inlaid card table, New York, circa 1780-1800. A very choice example of a type often erroneously accredited to Baltimore but known to have been made in New York. The inlaid top is expertly done and the bellflowers in the apron are a delightful touch. This table, with all its elegance, does not have the delicacy of the example illustrated below.

BEST

Hepplewhite mahogany inlaid card table, Baltimore, circa 1780-1800. One of the great masterpieces produced during the Baltimore Renaissance after the Revolutionary War.

Above. Detail of urn (see table at left). Credit would be given to the few fine craftsmen of today who could copy this masterful inlaid urn, but the tribute to the eighteenth century craftsman who created it must be far greater.

BEST

Left. Hepplewhite mahogany inlaid card table, Baltimore, circa 1780-1800. The double line inlay of the apron is worthy of study. Note how the corners meet at a 45° angle as they do in any fine eighteenth century example.

GOOD

Sheraton mahogany card table, Salem, Mass., circa 1800. A table of average quality. The legs are too thick for a table of this size. The proportions would be improved if the legs had more height and the table had more width.

BEST

Sheraton mahogany card table, carved by Samuel McIntire, Salem, Mass., circa 1800. An important table of fine proportions, which excels the table shown above even if the carving were eliminated. The finely carved basket of fruit and the waterleaf carving at the corners are typical motifs used by McIntire.

BETTER

Sheraton mahogany and satinwood card table with three-paneled front, Salem, Mass., circa 1800. A mediocre specimen of a fine type shown in its full stature by the table illustrated below. While these two tables evince casual similarities, the difference in execution and results is striking. This table does not have the breadth or grace of the other. The inept reeded leg does not have sufficient height and the reeding begins and ends nowhere, instead of being contained by moldings as in the better example.

BEST

Sheraton mahogany and satinwood card table with three-paneled front, Salem, Mass., circa 1800. An outstanding table of fine proportions and expert detail. Note the excellent bulbous reeded leg with the pleasing turning above the reeding. The oval of mahogany in the center provides contrast and refinement.

BEST

Sheraton mahogany and satinwood card table, Salem, Mass., circa 1800. An American classic of great delicacy and fine form. Note the magnificent figure of the flame satinwood. One of the best of the Salem card tables.

BEST

Sheraton mahogany sofa table, by Duncan Phyfe, New York, circa 1800-1815. A masterpiece of exceptional merit and great rarity. One of the few sofa tables produced in America, it is of Phyfe's distinctive design but shows unusual delicacy even for the master. The important acanthus-carved, urn-shaped supports avoid any semblance of heaviness. The reeded edge adds lightness to the top which has beautiful clover-leaf-shaped drop leaves.

GOOD

Sheraton mahogany card table, American, circa 1800-1815. An inferior table with boxy top and short stumpy legs.

BETTER

Sheraton mahogany card table, New York, circa 1800-1815. A good table, but far from outstanding. The turned pedestal is shapeless, the legs have too much of a hump and a short section of acanthus carving would have been better eliminated.

BEST

Sheraton satinwood card table, by Duncan Phyfe, New York, circa 1800-1815. One of a very few tables by Duncan Phyfe made entirely of satinwood. It exhibits every desirable feature for which Phyfe is justly famous, such as the fine clover-leaf-shaped top and the acanthus-carved urn pedestal.

GOOD

Sheraton mahogany four-column card table, New York, circa 1800-1815. An inferior table of the same general form as that of the tables shown below, but lacking the master's touch. There were many craftsmen in and around New York who imitated Duncan Phyfe, but few approached his ability or his standards. In this table the columns are too close together and too high, giving the table a top-heavy appearance.

Detail of base of Duncan Phyfe card table. A close-up of the fine acanthus leaf carving which was used extensively by Duncan Phyfe and helps to identify his work.

BEST

Pair of Sheraton mahogany card tables, by Duncan Phyfe, New York, circa 1800-1815. These represent Phyfe's best handiwork and are among the finest examples of Phyfe furniture in existence. Their superiority to the other table is quite apparent.

GOOD

Sheraton mahogany lyre-base card table, New York, circa 1815. A grotesque specimen which may have been conceived by someone whose nightmare of sea monsters was fresh in mind. If rarity were the primary factor in creating value, this table would be valuable. Since it is worthless from a collector's standpoint, it proves rarity only is a factor among examples of merit. The lyre is too massive at the base and too narrow above to support the top with its crude edge. The legs, with thin ugly carving, do not have enough flare to balance the wide top, giving a top-heavy appearance to the table.

BEST

Sheraton mahogany lyre-base card table, attributed to Duncan Phyfe, New York, circa 1800-1815. A choice table of excellent form, in which the craftsman used veneer on the lyre instead of carving.

BEST

Hepplewhite mahogany and satinwood corner washstand, Boston or Salem, Mass., circa 1780. A table of prosaic function lifted to exalted heights by a craftsman of genius and great scope. The beautifully scalloped crest and apron, sustained by the slender flaring legs and vertical spade feet, effect a unique form of exquisite perfection. The oval panel of flame satinwood relieves the monotony of an otherwise broad plain surface.

RESTORATIONS, REPLACEMENTS AND IMPERFECTIONS

RESTORATIONS, REPLACEMENTS AND IMPERFECTIONS

THIS chapter attempts to divide into two main categories—major and minor—those restorations or imperfections found in all genuine seventeenth and eighteenth century furniture. A major restoration or imperfection is one which eliminates a piece from consideration by discriminating collectors, therefore placing the piece in a substantially lower price bracket. A minor restoration is one which does not reduce the value or standing in its class of a piece.

This is a difficult chapter to write, for one must make certain arbitrary decisions, and being arbitrary is far from my intention. The difficulties of classification are obvious—the objects are all individual creations, and therefore each is different from the other. Then, too, the types of damages to which these creations have been subjected are manifold. But the fact is that in spite of the difficulties these restorations can be and are being classified and evaluated by dealers and collectors.

To my knowledge, however, there has not appeared in print any comprehensive effort to classify damages to antiques, and this chapter is an attempt to fill the gap. That there will be disagreement or controversy regarding specific classifications I have no doubt, for there are quite naturally differences in opinion and in evaluation among qualified dealers and experts in this field. But these differences are not fundamental. These same experts, who might validly dispute specific classifications in this chapter, would not dispute their general portent, since the classifications and the major restorations listed thereunder are basic.

Every type of furniture is composed of a certain few basic parts that are essential to the structure and design of that type. It is, therefore, possible and, I believe, feasible to list the basic parts of each general type and to list the major damages or restorations to these basic parts which are inherent to the type. The purpose of this is not to enable a collector to evaluate restorations of an antique and therefore to buy on his own judgment. Considerable experience and observation are primarily important. But a classification such as this—in fact, a book such as this—can serve several purposes: it can serve as a guide, to avoid obvious mistakes (it may help some collector to know, for example, that the replacement of the top of a drop leaf or Pembroke table eliminates the table from the collector's class no matter how desirable the base); it can show that the evaluation of antique furniture is scientific and not hit-and-miss as many people believe: it can also show that damages, defects, crudities, and imperfections are shunned, not sought after, by intelligent antique collectors.

If I were asked to give in one sentence the description of a premium piece of Early American furniture, I would say it was *a well-preserved successful example of an important school of colonial craftsmanship*. The purpose of the previous portions of the book is to demonstrate by comparison the successful examples of each important school. The purpose of this chapter is to demonstrate when an example is considered well preserved. I wish I could state that if a piece passes both these tests it is necessarily worthy of the most discriminating collection, but as in most attempts at oversimplification, I would be omitting an all-important factor, that of patina or color. I have not emphasized it in this book because the black and white photography does not show up the varying tones and qualities of color which add to the charm and beauty, as well as the value, of an antique. But I can at this point emphasize its importance. A large part of the desirability of antique furniture is determined by the patina (or surface color), which affects an antique-lover in much the same manner as the mellow taste of a well-aged wine affects a gourmet. Like the mellowness of old wine, the radiant patina of a fine piece of furniture cannot be simulated. Many of our great treasures were abused by the indiscriminate use of sandpaper, scraping, or harsh chemicals, resulting in the inestimable loss of that patina which only the patient centuries can bestow. It scarcely needs to be mentioned that such pieces are worth but a fraction of the value of those that have retained their mellow patina. The soft woods, with pine predominating, generally used in the interior construction of American pieces acquired an unmistakable tobacco-brown color through the centuries which cannot be successfully imitated by staining or other artificial methods. Genuine antiques of American make are therefore much more easily recognized than are corresponding English pieces which favored oak and other hard woods in the interior construction.

In *each type described in this section all the basic parts must be essentially original and intact in order that the piece be considered as premium by collectors.*

BED

Basic Parts

1. The two head posts.
2. The two foot posts.
3. The two long rails.
4. The two short rails.
5. The headboard.

Major Restorations

1. Loss of both long rails or both short rails.
2. Loss of original headboard.
3. Re-turning, re-reeding, or re-carving of foot posts. Since a bed with slender turned posts is more valuable than a heavier example, many beds have been given a slenderizing treatment. Such a bed would not be considered a collector's piece.

BUREAU

Basic Parts

1. The case.
2. The drawers.
3. The top.
4. The feet.

Note: The amount of restoration or replacement of the feet of a bureau, desk, chest-on-chest or secretary varies according to the type of foot, its relative importance in the integral design, and the availability of more perfect specimens. For instance, the loss of one claw and ball foot is major, the loss of one or even two bracket back feet is sometimes minor, but the loss of a front foot of any type is usually major. The judgment in any such case should be left to a qualified expert.

Major Restorations

1. Replacement or loss of the feet.
2. Changing or altering shape or size of case; making block front from straight front; bow front from straight front; small bureau from large one.
3. Replacement of top.
4. Replacement of one or more drawers or drawer fronts.
5. Embellishment of any portion by addition of inlay, veneer or carving.

CHAIR, SIDE

Basic Parts

1. The seat frame.
2. The front legs.
3. The stretchers, if any.
4. The back legs and posts.
5. The splat (or vertical or horizontal rungs).
6. The crest rail.

Major Restorations

1. Replacement, loss or splicing of one or more legs, front or back.
2. Serious restoration or reshaping of seat frame.
3. Loss or replacement of all the stretchers. (Replacement of a stretcher can often be overlooked.)
4. Replacement or loss of splat.
5. Replacement or loss of crest rail.
6. Embellishment of any portion of chair by addition of carving or inlay.

CHAIR, ARM

Basic Parts

1-6. Same as side chair.
7. The arms and arm supports.

MAJOR RESTORATIONS

1-6. Same as side chair.
7. Replacement, loss or serious restoration of arms or arm supports.
8. Addition of arms to a side chair.

CHAIR, MARTHA WASHINGTON

BASIC PARTS

1. The seat frame.
2. The legs.
3. The stretchers, if any.
4. The arms and arm supports.
5. The back posts.
6. The crest rail.

MAJOR RESTORATIONS

1. Replacement, loss or splicing of one or more legs.
2. Serious restoration of seat frame.
3. Loss or replacement of all the stretchers.
4. Replacement, loss or serious restoration of arms or arm supports.
5. Replacement or reshaping of crest rail.
6. Embellishment of legs, arms or arm supports by addition of carving or inlay.

CHAIR, WING

BASIC PARTS

1. The seat frame.
2. The legs.
3. The stretchers, if any.
4. The back posts.
5. The arms.
6. The wings.
7. The crest rail.

MAJOR RESTORATIONS

1. Replacement, loss or splicing of one or more legs.
2. Serious restoration of seat frame.
3. Loss or replacement of all the stretchers, if any.
4. Replacement or serious restoration of the arms or the wings.
5. Reshaping of wings.
6. Replacement or reshaping of crest rail.
7. Embellishment of legs by addition of carving or inlay.

CHAIR, WINDSOR

BASIC PARTS

1. The turned legs.
2. The turned stretchers.
3. The seat.
4. The arms and arm supports, if any.
5. The spindles and the crest rail.

MAJOR RESTORATIONS

1. Replacement, loss or splicing, or shortening of one or more legs.
2. Replacement of the turned stretchers.
3. Reshaping of seat or serious restoration of seat.
4. Replacement, loss or serious restoration of arms, arm supports or spindles.
5. Replacement, re-scrolling or re-shaping of crest rail.

CHEST-ON-CHEST

BASIC PARTS

1. The upper case section.
2. The lower case section.
3. The drawers.
4. The feet.

MAJOR RESTORATIONS

1. Replacement or loss of the feet.
2. Placing a bonnet or broken arch on a straight-top chest-on-chest, or reducing the size.
3. Loss or replacement of broken arch top or bonnet top.
4. Changing shape of drawer fronts, i.e., making block-front or serpentine-front base from straight-front base.

5. Assembly of an eighteenth century top on an eighteenth century base if the two sections did not originally begin life together.

CLOCK, GRANDFATHER

Basic Parts

1. The case.
2. The door.
3. The hood.
4. The dial.
5. The brass works.

Major Restorations

1. Serious restoration or alteration of case.
2. Replacement, loss or alteration of door.
3. Replacement or serious restoration of hood.
4. Replacement or substitution of the original dial or the later inscription of a maker's name to enhance the value of the clock.
5. Replacement, loss, substitution or serious restoration of the original brass works.
6. Embellishment of any portion of the case by addition of inlay, carving, fretwork, etc.

CLOCK, BANJO

Basic Parts

1. The case.
2. The lower painted glass panel and frame.
3. The upper painted glass panel and frame.
4. The dial.
5. The door.
6. The brass works.
7. The brass side pieces.

Major Restorations

1. Replaced, lost, cracked or repainted upper or lower painted glass panel, or both. The painted glass panels are certainly the most important parts of any banjo clock, and they must be genuine for the clock to be considered by collectors.
2. Replacement or serious restoration of frames bordering the glass panels.
3. Serious restoration of case.
4. Replacement or loss of original dial.
5. Replacement or loss of original brass works.
6. Replacement or loss of brass side pieces or brass door.
7. Later inscription of a maker's name.

CLOCKS, SHELF OR MANTEL

Basic Parts

1. The lower case section.
2. The upper case section (including the door).
3. The dial.
4. The brass works.
5. The glass painting, if any.
   Note: The glass painting generally occurs in the lower section of the clocks made in the first few decades of the nineteenth century. They also are conventional in the clocks by Eli Terry and his contemporaries.

Major Restorations

1. Serious restoration of upper or lower case section; loss or replacement of either; embellishment with inlay which was not there originally.
2. Replacement or loss of original dial.
3. Later inscription of a maker's name.
4. Replacement or loss of original brass works.

DESK, SLANT TOP

Basic Parts

1. The case section.
2. The feet.

3. The drawers.
4. The lid.
5. The interior drawers and compartments.

MAJOR RESTORATIONS

1. Replacement or loss of the feet.
2. Changing or altering the shape or size of case, i.e., making block front from straight front.
3. Replacement of one or more drawers or drawer fronts.
4. Replacement of slant lid.
5. Embellishment or improvement of original interior.

DESK, TAMBOUR

BASIC PARTS

1. The lower case section.
2. The legs or feet.
3. The drawers.
4. The upper case section.
5. The interior drawers and compartments.
6. The tambour slides.

MAJOR RESTORATIONS

1. Alteration or serious restoration of upper or lower case section.
2. Replacement or splicing of one or more legs.
3. Replacement of interior drawers or compartments.
4. Loss or replacement of tambour slides.
5. Embellishment by addition of inlay or veneer.
6. Replacement of drawers of lower case section.

LOWBOY, WILLIAM AND MARY

BASIC PARTS

1. The case section.
2. The top.
3. The drawers.
4. The turned legs.
5. The flat stretchers.
6. The ball feet.

MAJOR RESTORATIONS

1. Replacement or loss of turned legs, stretchers or feet. With a William and Mary lowboy, this restoration is the most frequent, since the underpinnings are fragile.
2. Replacement of top.
3. Re-veneering of top or drawer fronts.
4. Loss or replacement of one or more drawers.

LOWBOY, QUEEN ANNE OR CHIPPENDALE

BASIC PARTS

1. The case section.
2. The drawers.
3. The legs.
4. The top.

MAJOR RESTORATIONS

1. Replacement or splicing of one or more legs.
2. Replacement of top.
3. Changing shape of scrolled apron.
4. Replacement of one or more drawers.
5. Embellishment by addition of carving on knees or center drawer.

HIGHBOY, WILLIAM AND MARY

BASIC PARTS

1. The upper case section.
2. The lower case section.
3. The drawers.
4. The turned legs.
5. The flat shaped stretchers.
6. The ball feet.

MAJOR RESTORATIONS

1. Replacement or loss of turned legs, stretchers or feet. This is the most common restoration, since the legs were merely doweled into the frame, and with two hundred and fifty years of usage it is remarkable that so many intact examples have been discovered. Still, for every intact example, there are dozens

of restored specimens which are prized beyond their actual worth.

2. Assembly of an old top on an old base if the two sections did not begin life together.
3. Loss or replacement of veneered fronts if the highboy was originally veneered. If the highboy originally had drawer fronts veneered with burl walnut or maple or herringbone walnut, this veneer must be relatively intact. Small segments of veneer missing are of minor importance.

HIGHBOY, QUEEN ANNE OR CHIPPENDALE

Basic Parts

1. The upper case section.
2. The lower case section.
3. The four legs.
4. The drawers.

Major Restorations

1. The replacement of any one or more legs.
2. Splicing of one or more legs.
3. Embellishment of the legs, apron or center drawers by addition of carving.
4. Reshaping of the apron.
5. Assembly of an old top on an old base if the two sections did not begin life together. The upper and lower sections must have been made together and not joined later; no matter how good the match, it is misrepresentation for a dealer to sell an assembled highboy as genuine.
6. Converting a flat-top highboy to a bonnet top.
7. Replacement or loss of a bonnet top if one was originally present.

MIRROR, QUEEN ANNE

Basic Parts

1. The two-sectioned beveled glass.
2. The moldings.
3. The scrolled crest.
4. The carved shell, if any.

Major Restorations

1. Loss or replacement of either the upper or lower glass.
2. New or rescrolled crest.
3. Any embellishment, such as a carved shell in the crest, which was not present originally.
4. Loss or replacement of carved shell if one was there originally.

MIRROR, CHIPPENDALE

Basic Parts

1. The frame.
2. The scrolled ears.
3. The scrolled crest.
4. The scrolled base.

Major Restorations

1. More than two of the original scrolled ears.
2. Replacement or restoration of the scrolled base.
3. Replacement, or restoration or re-scrolling of the scrolled crest.
4. Replacement or loss of gilded bird or shell in crest if one was there originally.
5. Embellishment with a gilded bird or shell in crest if one was not there originally.
6. Loss or replacement of one or both side draperies if they were present originally.

MIRROR, CHIPPENDALE—CONSTITUTION OR MARTHA WASHINGTON TYPE

Basic Parts

1. The frame.
2. The carved and gilded scroll.
3. The carved and gilded side draperies.
4. The carved and gilded superimposed bird or other ornament.

Major Restorations

1. Replacement or loss of one or both side draperies.
2. Replacement or loss of the scrolled crest or the carved and gilded moldings.
3. Replacement or loss of the carved and gilded bird or other ornament.
4. Replacement or loss of scrolled base.

MIRROR, HEPPLEWHITE

Basic Parts

1. The frame.
2. The carved and gilded side flowers.
3. The carved and gilded urn.
4. The scrolled crest.
5. The scrolled base.

Major Restorations

1. Replacement or loss of the original side ornaments or flowers.
2. Replacement or loss of the original urn.
3. Replacement or serious restoration of the scrolled crest.
4. Replacement or loss of scrolled base.
5. Replacement or loss of painted glass panel, if one was present originally.

MIRROR, SHERATON

Basic Parts

1. The gilded frame.
2. The painted glass panel.

Major Restorations

1. Mutilated frame.
2. Lost, replaced or broken painted glass panel.
3. Lost or replaced superstructure, if any.

SECRETARY, QUEEN ANNE OR CHIPPENDALE

Basic Parts

1. The upper case section.
2. The lower case section.
3. The doors.
4. The drawers.
5. The scroll or bonnet top, if any.
6. The feet.

Major Restorations

1. Assembly of top and base if the two sections did not begin life together.
2. Replacement or loss of scroll or bonnet top if one was there originally.
3. The addition of a scroll or bonnet top to an originally flat-top secretary.
4. The replacement or loss of the doors.
5. The embellishment of the interior of the upper or lower section. Many blocked interiors with fans or carving began life much more simply. Not every elaborate interior should be suspect, but it should at least speak for itself and radiate genuineness.
6. The changing of the shape of the drawer fronts from straight front to the more valuable block front or serpentine front.
7. Loss or replacement of the feet.

SECRETARY, HEPPLEWHITE AND SHERATON

Basic Parts

1. The lower case section with the drawers.
2. The feet or legs.
3. The upper case section with the glass doors.
4. The scrolled crest.

Major Restorations

1. Assembly of the upper and lower case sections if they did not begin life together.
2. Loss or replacement of the doors.
3. Loss or replacement of the feet or splicing of legs.
4. Loss or replacement of one or more large drawers.
5. Loss or replacement of the scrolled crest.
6. Re-veneering, re-inlaying or embellishing with new inlay which was not present on the original piece.

SIDEBOARD

Basic Parts

1. The case.
2. The drawers.
3. The cupboard doors.
4. The top.
5. The legs.

Major Restorations

1. Replacement of one or more legs.
2. One or more legs spliced, built up, or shortened.
3. The case reduced in size or the shape of sideboard changed in any way.
4. Replacement of one or more drawers or cupboard doors.
5. Replacement of top.
6. Embellishment of inlay which was not present when the sideboard was made.

SOFA

Basic Parts

1. The back frame.
2. The wings or arms and arm supports.
3. The seat frame.
4. The legs.
5. The stretchers, if any.

Major Restorations

1. Loss, replacement or reshaping of crest rail, arms, wings or seat frame.
2. Loss or replacement of the stretchers, if any.
3. Embellishment of legs, arms or crest rail with carving or inlay which was not there originally.
4. Replacement, loss or splicing of one or more front legs.

TABLE, EARLY SIDE AND TAVERN

Basic Parts

1. The turned legs.
2. The feet.
3. The stretchers.
4. The frame.
5. The drawer, if any.
6. The top.

Major Restorations

1. Loss or replacement of the feet.
2. Replacement of one or more legs or stretchers.
3. Replacement of the drawer, if any.
4. Replacement, loss or reshaping of top.

TABLE, EARLY BUTTERFLY

Basic Parts

1. The turned legs and feet.
2. The stretchers.
3. The butterfly wings.
4. The frame.
5. The top and the two leaves.
6. The drawer, if any.

Major Restorations

1. Replacement of one or both leaves, or the whole top.
2. Replacement or loss of the turned legs, feet or stretchers.
3. Replacement or loss of the butterfly wings.
4. Replacement of the drawer, if any.

TABLE, EARLY GATELEG

Basic Parts

1. The turned legs.
2. The gates.
3. The stretchers.
4. The feet.
5. The frame.
6. The top, including the two drop leaves and the drawer, if any.

Major Restorations

1. Replacement or loss of the feet.
2. Replacement of one or more legs, stretchers, or gates.

3. Replacement or loss of the top or one or both drop leaves.

TABLE, TRIPOD

Basic Parts

1. The pedestal.
2. The three cabriole legs.
3. The birdcage section, if any.
4. The top.

Major Restorations

1. Reshaping or re-carving of the pedestal.
2. Replacement, loss or splicing of one or more legs. Carving an originally plain knee.
3. Assembly of an old top on an old base if the two did not begin life together.
4. Re-carving the edge of an old top from a plain edge to a dishrim or piecrust edge.
5. Loss or replacement of the top.

TABLE, QUEEN ANNE AND CHIPPENDALE DROP LEAF

Basic Parts

1. The frame.
2. The legs.
3. The top, including the drop leaves.

Major Restorations

1. Replacement, loss or splicing of one or more legs.
2. Serious restoration of frame.
3. Replacement or loss of top or one or more leaves; reshaping of leaves.
4. Assembly of an old top and an old base if the two did not begin life together.

TABLE, PEMBROKE

Basic Parts

1. The frame.
2. The legs.
3. The top, including the drop leaves.
4. The drawer, if any.
5. The stretchers, if any.

Major Restorations

1. Assembly of an old top and an old base if the two did not begin life together.
2. Replacement or loss of the original top or a drop leaf.
3. Reshaping of leaves.
4. Replacement, loss or splicing of one or more legs.
5. Replacement of the drawer, if one was present originally.
6. Embellishment of inlay on the legs, drawer front or top if this inlay was not there originally.
7. Loss or replacement of cross stretchers if these stretchers were there originally. This is of interest primarily on Chippendale Pembroke tables, since few fine Hepplewhite or Sheraton tables were made with stretchers.
8. Placing of cross stretchers where there were none originally.

TABLE, QUEEN ANNE AND CHIPPENDALE TEA

Basic Parts

1. The frame.
2. The legs.
3. The top.
4. The raised tray edge, if any.

Major Restorations

1. Replacement, loss or splicing of one or more legs.
2. Reshaping of the apron or skirt.
3. Replacement or loss of top.
4. Replacement or loss of raised tray edge if one was there originally.
5. Addition of a raised tray edge if there was none originally.
6. Reshaping of top if it is other than rectangular.

TABLE, BEDSIDE OR WORK

Basic Parts

1. The body.
2. The drawer or drawers.
3. The top.
4. The legs.

Major Restorations

1. Replacement, loss or splicing of one or more legs.
2. Slenderizing, re-reeding or re-carving Sheraton turned legs; re-inlaying of Hepplewhite square tapered legs.
3. Re-veneering of drawer fronts or sides of table.
4. Serious restoration to drawers or frame.
5. Replacement, loss or reshaping of original top.

TABLE, QUEEN ANNE AND CHIPPENDALE CARD

Basic Parts

1. The frame, including the drawer, if any.
2. The legs.
3. The top.
4. The folding leaf.

Major Restorations

1. Replacement, loss or splicing of one or more legs.
2. Serious restoration to frame or replacement of drawer.
3. Replacement or loss of top or folding leaf.
4. Addition of carving on knees if none was present originally.

TABLE, HEPPLEWHITE AND SHERATON CARD

Basic Parts

1. The frame.
2. The veneered front.
3. The legs.
4. The top.
5. The folding leaf.

Major Restorations

1. Serious restoration to frame.
2. Replacement, loss or splicing of one or more legs.
3. Re-reeding, re-turning or slenderizing the legs; embellishing them with carving or inlay which was not there originally.
4. Replacement or loss of top or folding leaf.
5. Re-veneering or re-inlaying the front or sides of the frame.